SPIRITUAL GROWTH FOR WOMEN

Self-Care Guidance, Beating Depression, & Secret Habits for Spiritual Blocks & Boundaries

ANGELA GRACE

© **Copyright 2021 - Ascending Vibrations - All rights reserved.**

The content contained within this book may not be reproduced, duplicated or transmitted without direct written permission from the author or the publisher.

Under no circumstances will any blame or legal responsibility be held against the publisher, or author, for any damages, reparation, or monetary loss due to the information contained within this book, either directly or indirectly.

Legal Notice:

This book is copyright protected. It is only for personal use. You cannot amend, distribute, sell, use, quote or paraphrase any part, or the content within this book, without the consent of the author or publisher.

Disclaimer Notice:

Please note the information contained within this document is for educational and entertainment purposes only. All effort has been executed to present accurate, up to date, reliable, complete information. No warranties of any kind are declared or implied. Readers acknowledge that the author is not engaged in the rendering of legal, financial, medical or professional advice. The content within this book has been derived from various sources. Please consult a licensed professional before attempting any techniques outlined in this book.

By reading this document, the reader agrees that under no circumstances is the author responsible for any losses, direct or indirect, that are incurred as a result of the use of the information contained within this document, including, but not limited to, errors, omissions, or inaccuracies.

CONTENTS

Claim Your bonuses below	v
Introduction	xi

1. ARE YOUR THOUGHTS RUINING YOUR LIFE? — 1
   Escaping the Spiral of Destructive Thoughts — 3

2. DON'T JUST BECOME SUCCESSFUL, BECOME WHOLE — 10
   Set Your Priorities Straight — 12

3. THE SHORTCUT TO BYPASS NEGATIVE ENERGETIC INFLUENCES AND AWAKEN SPIRITUALLY — 18
   Let Go of Your Ego — 20

4. LOOK AT YOUR LIFE AND BE HONEST.... ARE YOU READY TO LET GO OF WHAT NO LONGER SERVES YOU? — 26
   Clear Your Aura from Negativity — 29

5. DIVINE FEMININE ENERGY AND HOW TO STOP CARING WHAT OTHER PEOPLE THINK OF YOU — 35
   Stop Caring About What Other People Think of You — 38

6. CORD CUTTING, RELEASING SPIRITUAL BLOCKS, THE BEAUTY OF FORGIVENESS AND SPIRITUAL CLEANSING — 44
   Aligning Your Chakras — 46

7. SPIRITUAL HEALING, CRUSHING DEPRESSION, SETTING BOUNDARIES, AND HOW TO STOP LIVING IN DYSFUNCTION — 52
   Beating Depression — 54

8. EMPOWER YOURSELF, EMPOWER YOUR FAMILY — 62
   Putting Yourself First — 64

9. PERSEVERANCE, DISCIPLINE, AND
EMPOWERMENT FOR THE SPIRITUALLY
POWERFUL WOMAN (DON'T QUIT!)   70
On the Path of Spiritual Growth   73

10. AMAZING GUIDED MEDITATIONS TO
SUPERCHARGE YOUR SPIRITUAL GROWTH   79
Guided Meditation to Accomplish Wholeness   80
Guided Meditation for Cleansing Chakras   82
Guided Meditation for Mastering Perseverance   84
Guided Meditation for Spiritual Growth   86
Guided Meditation to Overcome Fear   88

11. THE 30-MINUTE DAILY EMPOWERMENT
RITUAL FOR SPIRITUAL GROWTH   91
The 30-Minute Spiritual Growth Daily Ritual Secret
Formula   93

Afterword   103
References   107
Your Feedback is Valued   111
Your Bonus Audiobook is Ready   113

CLAIM YOUR BONUSES BELOW

To help you on your spiritual journey, we've created some free bonuses to help you clear energetic baggage that no longer serves you and manifest a life that suits you better. Bonuses include a companion video course that includes over 4.5 hours of empowering content, energy-tapping videos, powerful guided meditations, journals, and more.

You can get immediate access by going to the link below or scanning the QR code with your cell phone.

https://bonus.ascendingvibrations.net

Free Bonus #1: The 3-Step Chakra Tune-Up Course
Want to know a unique way to target the chakras? Elevate Your Existence by Targeting the Subconscious, the Physical, & the Spiritual

- Discover a unique 3-step chakra targeting method that so many people aren't taking advantage of!
- Hack your brain, elevate body, mind, and spirit, and release blocks holding you back from greatness
- Awaken amazing energy to tailor a reality that suits you better
- Stop wasting precious time on ineffective methods

Free Bonus #2: The Manifesting Secret Formula Toolkit
Are you done with settling in life, wasting precious time, and ready to attract your highest potential to you?

Free Bonus #3: The Spiritual Cleansing Toolkit
Are you ready to drop all of the negative energy that no longer serves you?

- Release energetic blocks that could be causing imbalances

- Awaken amazing energy to supercharge your aura
- Create a beautifully cleansed, energetic environment

Free Bonus #4: A Powerful 10-Minute Energy Healing Guided Meditation

All of these amazing bonuses are 100% free. You don't need to enter any details except for your email address. To get instant access to your bonuses, go to

https://bonus.ascendingvibrations.net

INTRODUCTION

Do you want to supercharge your spiritual growth and see what happens? Are you wondering what your life would be like if you listened to that voice inside you that keeps asking you to dig deeper? If you are anything like me, you must have already looked through books and articles about spirituality, energy healing, and divine feminine energy. Maybe this is the first time you are reading one of my books or maybe we have crossed paths before. If it's the former, I am so glad you have made it here—if it's the latter, I am truly bursting with pride and joy because you have trusted me again.

Spiritual growth is a huge topic that involves many different aspects of your life. However, it is a matter that inspires everyone in the world. How can anyone be satisfied and fulfilled in their life, not knowing what lies ahead for them on the other side of their reality? Many people waste their life consumed in here and now, instead of discovering more about their being. Even though temporary pleasures can be fun, they do not last. They leave you with a yearning for more. This yearning only grows stronger as we mature.

Unless you delve into the mysteries of spirituality, you can never feel whole in your life. This is a given. You might achieve some goals of yours and this might make you feel proud, accomplished, success-

INTRODUCTION

ful, or even happy. Yet, all those feelings will eventually fade away and you will be left there craving for more. As you are lying in bed trying to sleep at night, you will realize that nothing matters. You had it all wrong this entire time. What matters is that you find your life's purpose and dedicate your life to it. You must get out of your comfort zone and strive for your goals. More than that, you need to decide if you are willing to labor hard to reach your fullest potential or if you wish to compromise and spend the rest of your life in ignorance.

There is a wide misconception that has been driving people to pursue material success, rather than turn to their inner self and explore their endless possibilities. I know you have been thinking about it all this time. I am sure you have been studying the best way to shift your mindset and turn your life upside down. I am here to tell you that it is possible. You just need to let go of your past habits and implement new ones in their place. Rather than indulging in other people's demands all the time, you must set yourself as the top priority in your life. Instead of allowing those vampires out there to feast on your precious energy, you must set healthy boundaries and get rid of those around you who do not serve your life's purpose anymore.

If you want to attract amazing things in your life, you must set your priorities straight and dedicate every fiber of your being to bringing them to your reality. Have faith in the universal energy, as this is leading the way. At the same time, do your part and stick to your goals. No matter how challenging the endeavor, don't quit until you make it happen. You have endless power within yourself and therefore you need to persevere and remain true to your purpose, your higher calling. Don't get discouraged by the hardships, as they will forge your will and prepare you for the greatness that is just around the corner. Embrace your failures, embrace the obstacles that make it harder for you to reach your end destination. These obstacles only add to the value of your accomplishment.

INTRODUCTION

MY JOURNEY

Let's begin with a confession. I was not always like that in my life. I was not always happy, radiant with light and blissful. Life had taken its toll on me early on in my twenties when I tried to cope with many challenges. To be honest, I found it extremely difficult to maintain a healthy mindset as I strived through life. I was still at college, trying hard to make it to the finish line. At the same time, I had to find a job that paid the bills and somewhat made me feel good about myself. All that had ended up with me exhausted, unable to deliver my projects in time, and always calling in sick at work.

As I had taken on more than I could chew, I found myself in a difficult situation. I was underwater, gasping for air and at times I felt like letting go. Life was too cruel and I could not take it anymore. At my age, I always thought that I would enjoy every second of partying and having a great time with my friends. Never had I dreamed of a life where I would be overwhelmed by projects and deadlines that I kept failing. Luckily, I had an awesome network of support that never failed to lift me up and loved me, when I could not even love myself. However, I got on the verge of collapsing and I felt the daunting presence of depression as it crept silently into the room.

I cannot even begin to imagine what my life would be like if it hadn't been for those people around me. They lifted me up and carried me to a safe place, where I could feel calm. Eventually, I realized that I had to change my life and reevaluate my priorities. I relaxed a bit and allowed myself a little more time to finish college. My employer was actually very sympathetic when I explained the situation. People at work helped me by adjusting the entire schedule so that it would fit my own needs. I cannot thank them enough.

Spirituality has played an important role in my transformation. If I hadn't reached out to ask for guidance from a higher power, I know that I would not have been able to recover as quickly as I did.

INTRODUCTION

I was blessed to have a loving friend in my life back then, Linda. She is the person who introduced me to healing crystals and lit up a sparkle within me. Immediately, I fell in love with their beauty and I was drawn to them for the way they made me feel. They soothed my soul as I held them in my palms and they inspired me to pull through. From then on, I discovered not only crystals but also energy healing, and spirituality.

As I discovered my true life's purpose, I started writing books that revolve around spirituality. Over the years, I have had the pleasure and true honor to communicate with thousands of my readers and I would like to thank them for their trust and loyalty in me. In my books *Energy Healing Made Easy, Protect Your Energy, Crystals Made Easy, Feminine Energy Awakening, Manifesting for Women, and Reiki Made Easy*, I tried to pass on my knowledge and personal experience to other people. This is my calling, this is my life's purpose. I am meant to teach others and guide them as they get to experience their spiritual awakening.

After having discovered what I was meant to do in my life, everything suddenly fell into place. My everyday life became so much better and filled with content. I was able to get up in the morning smiling, rather than feel grumpy all day and get exhausted with only an hour at work. Instead, I felt pumped with energy and I feel the same way even now. Not a day goes by without giving thanks to the world for my blessings. I never forget where I came from and I never let anything or anyone deprive me of my own personal happiness.

Embark on a Unique Journey

I am so happy that you have chosen my book. I hope you find everything you need here so that you can initiate your journey towards spiritual growth. It is my privilege to guide you through this process and help shed light on several aspects of spirituality that are harder to digest. You may have hit a low in your life, just as I did. Perhaps you are on the verge of bursting with tears and giving up on your life goals. You shouldn't! You simply need to shift your mindset

INTRODUCTION

and create a welcoming environment to invite all those amazing things in your life, rather than settle for eternal suffering and incompletion.

By reading this book, you will gather all the information required to take that brave step and say "That's enough!" to anything or anyone standing in the way, preventing you from reaching your fullest potential. You will learn how to spot all those negative people whose life purpose is to drain you of your energy and distract you from your true calling. Do not be condescending with these people. They do not belong in your life. They are ruining everything you have worked so hard to accomplish and you should get out of there as soon as possible. It is important that you cut the cord early on in your life, so as to prevent being poisoned by their own negativity. See when it is time to walk away and don't feel guilty about that.

After settling the score with those energy vampires, you need to take an honest look at yourself from a distance. Are there any destructive thought patterns bringing you down? You are not alone in this and I will show you how you can escape this spiral. You will be encouraged to set your priorities straight, focusing not just on success. This can be misleading and end up distorting your reality. What you should be focusing on is wholeness. Only through this path of becoming whole can you experience absolute happiness and joy in your life.

In this book, you will also learn how to live in the present moment and how to ignite your divine feminine energy. There are practical exercises for you to try out so that you master the virtue of forgiveness and let go of your ego. You will also find out how to cleanse your aura and how to put yourself first before you can help others in their life. More than that, you will discover more about depression and how to get past this awfully negative emotion that keeps dragging people down. You will find all the necessary tools to take care of yourself, grow spiritually, and accomplish your goals gracefully. Finally, you will see the morning and nighttime rituals

xv

INTRODUCTION

that I have prepared for you so that you are always super energized and focused on meeting your goals for the day.

I am looking forward to embarking on this journey with you. Join me and let's explore the depths of spirituality together, in an experience you will never forget. Happy reading!

1

ARE YOUR THOUGHTS RUINING YOUR LIFE?

Are your thoughts standing in the way of your success? Do you often find yourself consumed by your own fears and insecurities? This problem is much more frequent and widespread than you would have imagined. In fact, most women have second-guessed or sabotaged themselves at least once in their lifetime. You might feel you don't deserve to get that promotion, you are not worthy of being loved, you are too fat or your life is an entire mess. When thinking like that, you are setting a self-fulfilling prophecy into motion. You hold an expectation or a belief that manifests into your life because you have allowed it to (Ackerman, 2018).

Self-sabotage constrains your life. It not only stops you from achieving what you want, but it also erodes your happiness and destroys your self-esteem. You are found in a self-inflicting trap, where you are harming no one but yourself. Instead of standing up for yourself, you cater to your insecurities and feed them with what they need to grow stronger. Unless you know what causes those destructive behaviors and how to deal with them, you cannot rewire your limiting beliefs about yourself. You avoid taking a look at your own personal issues and this takes its toll on your life.

When you are born, you have no beliefs. You absorb knowledge through empirical observation and you rely on those around you, in order to keep you safe and sound. You begin forming a belief system, turning to the environment around you for guidance. As a baby, you depend on the beliefs of your parents and close family. Growing up, you expand your environment and absorb beliefs from friends, teachers, the media, your neighbors, and the people you form relationships with.

Although you grow up thinking that you have no limits holding you back, the first time you attempt to do something out of the norm, your subconscious mind sends a shocking feeling to warn you. This negative emotion serves as a repellent and makes you confine yourself within the boundaries created by your belief system. In other words, you sabotage yourself by not achieving what you don't think you can achieve in the first place. You cannot break the boundaries of your beliefs.

As you develop self-awareness, you are able to realize the ways in which you sabotage yourself. Through this process, you can rewire your mind and make sure you modify the behavior that keeps holding you back. If you are determined to improve your life, it is imperative that you uncover any areas where you repeatedly fail. Where does life go wrong for you? Be honest and look at your existence with a critical eye. Notice your negative feedback and comments on these parts of your life.

After having defined the things you need to change, it is time to find their root cause. What has made you feel this way? What has triggered you to self-sabotage? To do that, you should go back to your childhood and trace any traumatic experiences from the past that are linked to your behavior. Moving forward, you need to prove your subconscious mind wrong. Master the skills that disprove your limiting beliefs. Become an expert in what you once thought was out of your reach.

By now, you know how to overcome self-limiting beliefs. Hopefully, by following the guidelines given below, you will be able to reprogram your mind. However, you should always remain vigilant of the threats that might emerge one day. Self-sabotage has defined your existence all this time. Therefore, it will continue trying to restore its past glory and creep back into your mind. To avoid all that, you need to enhance your self-awareness. You need to be aware of the threats so that they do not take control over you anymore.

ESCAPING THE SPIRAL OF DESTRUCTIVE THOUGHTS

Your thoughts can block creativity, sexuality (libido), sexual/creative energy, and many other elements that create a lust for life by freezing your nervous systems in a stressed fight or flight response. This can be caused by repetitive fear and trauma with your thoughts and worries. Until you unfreeze and clear this fear and pain, you are blocked from moving forward spiritually at your maximum potential.

Ever since antiquity, mankind has faced the fundamental urge to survive all kinds of dangers. Wild animals threatened to kill people in the old days, along with deadly diseases, war, and several other dangers. To that end, our body has adapted accordingly. This is why it has developed an instinctual way to keep us safe. When we encountered a pack of lions, for example, we would have three distinct reactions to choose from: fight, run away, or freeze. Of course, the outcome of each reaction varied greatly and determined whether or not we would live to see another day.

Fight, flight, or freeze reactions come naturally, so we do not

ANGELA GRACE

need to think about them. They turn off that part of our brain, so as to offer us an immediate response to that threat before us. So the prefrontal lobes of the brain get shut down, while the limbic brain gets amped up to boost our instinctive behavior. Imagine having to go through your options in detail and then make up your mind about how to deal with that pack of lions. It would be counterproductive, as you would most probably end up becoming their meal.

Along with our brain function, an imminent danger leads to several other reactions from your body. Blood gets forwarded from your extremities to your muscles because your body assumes you are going to need them. This is the reason why you often feel like having cold feet or sweaty palms, in cases of extreme anxiety. Your adrenaline glands get turned on so that you get a boost of energy when you most need it. After that, though, your body soon starts shaking.

More than that, your digestive system ceases to function. There is no point in digesting when faced with a danger that may eliminate you, is there? Your stomach feels bad and you lose your appetite. Your breath gets shorter and your muscles get tighter. Your immune system is also shut down, as your energy is focused on nothing else than survival. Unlike the fight or flight reactions, the freeze option makes you feel numb, shrink and hide from confrontation.

This mechanism we have created can be extremely useful to us in the dangers mentioned above, where small bursts of immense energy and adrenaline are required. However, nowadays there are no actual imminent dangers out there threatening our extinction. As a result, this instinct only makes us feel uncomfortable. We perceive something as physically dangerous, even though the truth is that we are entirely safe. For prolonged periods of time, this results in exhaustion and chronic fatigue, insomnia, digestive issues, muscle tension, and autoimmune diseases.

Freedom comes when you refuse to be victims to your thoughts and realize you have already been equipped with power from the universe (God) to fight and win the war for your mind. But first, let's

4

SPIRITUAL GROWTH FOR WOMEN

see how such destructive thoughts can occur. Where do they stem from? OCD is short for Obsessive-Compulsive Disorder. It can either cause obsessions over specific behavioral patterns or develop the urge to repeat the same actions (Fields, 2003). Those suffering from OCD will not feel at peace unless they follow the rules they have set religiously.

For instance, it is necessary for someone to turn on and off the lights four times when entering a room. If this doesn't happen, they will remain on edge and they will not be able to relax or let go. This pattern takes place non-stop, as the fear of what is about to happen otherwise is haunting. Even though some of these behavioral patterns may be deemed as superstitions and dealt with lightly, over time they become almost unbearable. The person suffering from such thoughts has to settle for a life that is greatly restricted in many ways.

Those thoughts that get stuck in your mind and govern your behavior are called "intrusive thoughts." Unlike what you might think, the truth is that people do not control their thoughts. The more you try to control what thoughts you are having, the more you are likely to suffer from unwanted thoughts. Take a moment and experiment with your thought control, by saying to your brain that it cannot think of the beach. Now close your eyes and notice closely. Are you thinking of the beach or are you thinking that you should not be thinking about the beach? I am guessing it is one of these options.

What you can control, though, is the decision of what to make of these thoughts. Once they pop into your head, how do you respond? If you take a deep breath and start looking at the big picture, you will end up soothing the intensity of the thoughts and eventually learn how to ignore them. In this way, you can master the art of letting go. You can develop a defense mechanism that allows you to live a normal life, without anxiety and without any obsessive thoughts getting over control. It might take some time and convincing, but in the end, you will be freed from these thoughts.

5

For instance, next time you feel compelled to repeat a specific phrase three times or any other "ritual" you have designed over the years, try to be rational. Ask yourself if it is going to help you in any way or affect your environment. Try to base your answer on facts, rather than your own intuition. It is highly likely that you will realize how futile it is to depend on something so trivial and unrelated to the actual outcome you are anticipating. You may ask yourself, "What happens in the universe if I blow my whistle four times in a row, every single time I leave the house? What impact does it have on reality for me to turn the lights off and back on again three times in a row?" If you give yourself the chance, you will see that your actions are interpreted correctly.

Get out of Toxic Thinking Patterns

Allow me to share something personal about my past. I used to suffer from OCD thoughts that ate me up from inside. No matter how good I was at my job, I used to think that external factors were to determine the course of my professional future. This started out subtly, as I began repeating a specific course of words every time the phone rang. Before I even answered the phone, I would have to repeat these words three times in a row. Then I would answer the phone, knowing that nothing negative could affect me. I had influenced the universe, so every phone call would be for my own benefit.

As I completed my ritual, I was convinced that it worked. I was glad that I had found this system, which helped me on my path to

SPIRITUAL GROWTH FOR WOMEN

success. Nevertheless, after a while, that was not enough. As soon as I received some bad news over the phone, I tried to rationalize it, and then I thought that I had to add something extra into the mix. From then on, I had to scratch the area between my right thumb and index while repeating these words. You can imagine how stressful and even painful it had become for me.

Over time, I had an epiphany and I knew I had to do something. After discussing it with my husband and my closest friends, I saw they were genuinely concerned about the way I behaved. In order to get rid of this obsession, I turned to EFT tapping. This was an easy-to-do ritual that I followed every day, so as to leverage the right tools towards cutting the cord with these intrusive thoughts of mine. Before I could even realize it, I was able to think straight and see through the mysterious ritual that held me captive all this time.

In my case, I managed to elevate my personal vibration and release the stagnant energy that had accumulated all this time within me. EFT tapping allowed me to focus on my own potential, instead of trying to figure out why external factors contributed to my personal success. It has been a life-changing experience for me and I continue following the very same ritual every now and then. Especially when I feel my insecurities creeping in slowly, I don't wait until they spread their claws.

One of the major causes of toxic thinking patterns is trauma. Post-traumatic stress disorder (PTSD) is a mental health condition that derives from a painful event of the past. When a patient suffers from trauma, they tend to bury it deep into their soul. No matter how deep it has been buried, though, there are times when it emerges to the surface. More specifically, there are triggers that awaken this trauma and this might lead to physical manifestations that are extremely hurtful (Mayo Clinic Staff, 2018).

Stress and fear get trapped in the body, as the patient does not have the capacity to respond efficiently to an imminent threat. Of course, this painful event does not affect everyone in the same way. For instance, two people who have survived a plane crash will not experience identical symptoms. They will deal with that tragic event in their own way. When a loved one passes away, it comes as a shock to us all. However, we do not go through the grieving stages in the same manner. This happens because we do not all have the same coping mechanisms, which help us process the perceived events.

Once people find themselves overwhelmed by emotions stemming from huge events like the ones pointed out above, it is of paramount importance to discharge the stored energy. Although releasing that tension will help them relax, they do not always act like that. Instead, they often interfere with this innate ability to overcome traumas and go through a successful healing process. Have you ever experienced similar negative emotions deriving from your body's inability to resolve those physical reactions?

Although I am going to refer to several of these techniques later on in the book, it is worth noting that there are many different options for you to choose from. Below, you can find a simple EFT tapping session that helps you reconnect with your body. To some, EFT tapping might not be the best approach. If you want to repel toxic thinking patterns, you can also experiment with TRE (trauma release exercises), meditation, and yoga.

A simple exercise offers you the opportunity to become more aware of your physical presence and your surroundings. Start by tapping the exterior part of your palm and repeat: "This is my hand." Follow the same ritual for every part of your body, changing the statement accordingly. In this way, you gain full ownership of your body. You become grounded and you experience a deep connection to the universe.

Another tool that you can use is your mirror. Whenever you are having negative emotions about something, take a moment and look at yourself in the mirror. As soon as you begin talking about this specific event that triggers anger, frustration, or disappointment, your body will start changing. Your jaw will become more clenched, your shoulders will go up and tighten, your look will be

SPIRITUAL GROWTH FOR WOMEN

more aggressive. Upon realizing that, you will be able to modify your bodily responses towards that negative emotion. Relax your muscles, release the tension and feel your body get rid of the stagnant energy.

Finally, use visualization to dispose of toxic thinking patterns. Close your eyes and visualize being absolutely serene. Picture yourself in a quiet place, a dreamy landscape where you would like to be. Picture it in every little detail, so that you can feel it with your senses and really be there. As you breathe deeply, think of everything that fills you with anger and brings out all these negative feelings. With every exhale, release the tension and imagine you are letting go of those emotions. When you feel lighter, you can open your eyes.

9

2

DON'T JUST BECOME SUCCESSFUL, BECOME WHOLE

Most people live their lives absorbed in their eagerness for success. They wish to thrive in their career, earn more money and buy all the things they have ever dreamed of. Of course, there is nothing wrong with that. Career and monetary success can be awesome and they certainly make your life easier. However, they should not be the end goal. Otherwise, sooner or later people realize that they are missing something. What about things that money cannot buy?

When you spend your life constantly in pursuit of success, you are in a state of wanting. You lack something and you do your best to meet that need of yours. Therefore, you feel as if you are deprived of something. Still, is this really what you should be feeling? Is success the most important aspect of your being? Take a moment and visualize that success. What emotions stem from that? How does success make you feel?

Once you do that, you will see that the things you have set your mind on achieving prove to be secondary. They are almost trivial and they soon fade away, giving their place to other needs of similar importance. Have you ever expressed your intent to become successful, by associating that accomplishment with the feeling of

SPIRITUAL GROWTH FOR WOMEN

happiness? "If I lose 20 pounds, I will be so happy!", "My life will be complete if I buy this house!", or "I will be over the moon if I go on a date with him!" Do any of these phrases ring a bell?

Oddly enough, you get to achieve one of these goals and you are happy for the shortest time frame. You celebrate your victory and get filled with all these wonderful emotions. Before you know it, maybe after a day or two, you start complaining and you realize that you have indeed idolized a state of being for no reason. By adding more value to your goal, you have ended up feeling frustrated by the outcome. This leads to a state of profound disappointment.

Unless you get rid of living in lack and separation, you can never be fulfilled in your life. You will try hard and you will succeed in doing things that make you happy for a while. Still, if you are after permanent bliss and content, you need to shift your mindset. It is essential that you remain focused on what actually matters. Obviously, temporary achievements are great and should be celebrated. No one claims that you should give up on such pleasures. It is of the essence, though, to maintain your internal aura independently of your environment.

No matter what the circumstances might be, knowing your higher calling allows you to be whole. You no longer depend on external factors to be happy. It doesn't matter if others approve of your decisions, your lifestyle, and the path you have chosen to follow. As long as you are certain of your choice through self-awareness and self-actualization, you do not find that approval vital for you. It is of course welcome, but it is not a prerequisite of your own happiness.

Most people in the world create their life matter to matter, experiencing all the hardships that come along. They get affected by negativity and they fail to enjoy every single day to the fullest. Instead, they are constantly craving for something else. Even right after accomplishing something great, they will subconsciously begin thinking of their next endeavor. Such an attitude is what brought mankind here, having developed a treasured civilization filled with technological wonders, innovations, and out-of-the-box thinking. However, on a personal level, such a behavioral pattern can be exhausting.

It is what you are feeling deep inside that gets projected to the world. If you continue feeling despair, lack, and envy, this is what you are going to reflect. In turn, this is what you are going to attract back in your life. According to the Law of Attraction, you are bound to receive the things that you emit to the world. If you are giving out low-energy emotions, this is what you are getting in return. As soon as you elevate your vibration and project positive emotions, you become a magnet and attract anything you want. This is a great transformation in your life, happening from within.

To that end, it is crucial that you change the process you have used so far and figure out how to experience wholeness. One of the core elements of wholeness is gratitude. You need to acknowledge your blessings. You have received a wealth of great things in your life and you should be conscious of them. Do not concentrate on the negative things that take place. Rather than reinforcing all this negativity, get rid of it through being grateful. Give thanks to the world, your family and loved ones, your colleagues and yourself, God, or any other higher power you believe in. Instead of wasting valuable energy trapped in negative emotions and toxic thoughts, let them go and fill yourself with gratitude.

SET YOUR PRIORITIES STRAIGHT

According to Carl Jung, the ultimate self-realization takes place when the unconscious is integrated into the conscious. This is called the Individualization Process and it is a quite complex concept. Let's see how it works. In the core of every individual lies their self, representing a blend of their unconscious and conscious entity. There are four main elements forming these two parts of the self: the ego, the persona, the shadow, and the animus or anima.

First of all, the ego is the image we have about ourselves. It is

SPIRITUAL GROWTH FOR WOMEN

the narrative we tell about ourselves, constantly growing as we grow. On the contrary, the persona is the mask we tend to wear towards conforming to society. It is dictated by norms and ethics. Moving forward, the shadow consists of unwanted characteristics we have. They are repressed, as they are negatively charged. Lastly, in every man, there is a woman residing deep inside the unconscious and vice versa. This is why men and women possess characteristics that are typically deemed respectively as feminine and masculine. Women have the animus and men have the anima.

The vast majority of the self is concealed within the unconscious and is partly impenetrable. Within this part that is out of reach, repressed memories and forgotten thoughts are found. Along with that, there is also the collective unconscious with memories that are identical for all people. In addition, there are also two archetypal figures within the unconscious. These figures can be found in dreams and feature concepts like the hero, the wizard, the great mother, and God. The archetypes do not have shapes of actual figures, but they reflect your unconscious and what lies hidden in there.

When Jung talked about the Individualization Process, he referred to the integration of unconscious parts of the psyche into the conscious. This in turn leads to the feeling of wholeness. Although most people achieve that through aging, there are several other methods to stimulate similar outcomes. During this process, the ego acknowledges that it is not the center of the self. The individual realizes that there are hidden parts of their personality in the dark places of the unconscious. By suppressing this part of the self, meaning the shadow, we essentially suppress life. The repercussions for doing that are devastating, as they can lead to dysfunctional neuroses (Jeffrey).

If you want to be happy, opt for a holistic approach to life. Do not reject any part of yourself, no matter how dark they are. They are all yours and it is important to remain conscious of your being. You cannot have a distorted image of yourself and still expect to

ANGELA GRACE

reach the highest levels of self-awareness. This cannot be. You will only prolong your misery, as you are feeling incomplete and you are missing out on your true purpose in life. Every day comes and goes, leaving you emptier inside.

Jung's process is a great method used to interpret existence. It takes into consideration several aspects of one's self, interpreting people's behavioral patterns. Every human being is complex and consists of both positive and negative traits. There is no point in concealing those parts of your personality you don't like. This will end ugly for you, as sooner or later they will emerge and create a domino effect in your life. What you should do is comprehend all the details, all the different aspects of yourself and try to reason with them. If you abhor a specific part of you, try to change it. But first, accept it—this is your reality.

There is a wake-up call for everyone to become conscious. It varies greatly from one person to the next. Such wake-up calls typically include huge changes in a person's everyday life. For instance, being diagnosed with severe disease or breaking up, getting divorced, or experiencing betrayal on various levels are all triggers that make you re-evaluate your priorities. These events are intense enough to provide a shock that awakens every single cell of your body.

Once the person experiences such a shocking event, they tend to look at their life from a distance. As a result, they are able to spot any dysfunctions and be critical of their past behavior. By considering their survival under extreme physical or emotional conditions as a blessing, it dawns on them that something has to change. Feeling whole suddenly becomes the number one priority for them, although up to that moment it was more or less neglected as a concept. They become more insightful, grounded, and at the same time connected to the bigger picture.

Upon passing through that threshold, people get more interested in what lies beneath the surface. It is like they are having an epiphany, where they gain the power to see clearly. Through this newly acquired superpower, they distance themselves from past mistakes and understand what needs to be done from now on. Along with that, they develop a deep interest in spirituality. Steering clear from distractions, they delve into the purest form of self-awareness, in pursuit of answers. Above all, they rely on universal energy; an energy that is much bigger than all of us and guides us towards the light.

Trust in the Universal Energy

I am sure you have experienced moments in your life when you feel absolutely aligned with the universe. You feel as if everything is exactly the way it was meant to be, appreciating the present moment and enjoying life to its fullest potential. This is pure bliss and it stems from a higher power. As pointed out earlier, God is an archetype that is present in all cultures around the world. Nobody questions the existence of something greater than us, something that governs the universe and showers us with love, care, and affection. Once you connect to this powerful source of infinite potential, you immediately experience a transformation beyond your wildest dreams.

Most people find it hard to trust. They have found the hard way that they need to depend solely on their powers. Maybe they have experienced betrayal, or they have realized that others never live up to their expectations or promises. Therefore, they tried hard to depend on themselves and no one else. Otherwise, they would feel uncomfortable. They would feel vulnerable, unable to control their

ANGELA GRACE

destiny. It is difficult to come to terms with such an acknowledgment.

However, trusting the higher power from above is actually liberating. It allows you to lift a huge burden off your chest. This burden has been weighing down on you, preventing you from living in the present moment and truly enjoying life. Once you discover that someone else is looking out for you and there is absolute harmony in the universe, things are starting to make sense.

It is vital that you establish a connection with this higher power. Whatever is blocking this connection should be dealt with, so that you can unlock endless possibilities in your life. Have faith in the universe and things are bound to work out in the end. If you keep questioning why you are not catching a break, why you are always tormented, and why you fail instead of thriving, you will be caught up in a vicious, never-ending cycle. This is the cycle of doubt and despair.

Of course, by trusting the universe you should not automatically decline responsibility for your actions. There are people who always blame destiny for the poor choices they make. Under that perspective, destiny is nothing more than an excuse for not resuming responsibility for your actions. You are on the path to success and the universe will always provide for you, but your actions are governed by you and you alone. If you select to act against your well-being, this is definitely going to impact you in the long run.

What you need to do is project goodness to the world. Through your actions, you must emit positive energy. This is going to come back to you, as the Law of Attraction dictates. Driven by the divine power within you, you should act in a way that promotes self-awareness. It is a simple yet powerful concept, that of cause and effect. Behave in a way you want others to behave to you. Give to the world, as this is what you have been meant to do. There is a hidden power within you, your true calling. Listen to that voice and be generous with others, giving back to humanity.

It is all about the energy you emit. Match the frequency of the reality you wish to see in your life so that you receive it without limits. You have been charged, just like all beings within the universe. Elevate this vibrational energy of yours and you will realize that good things will flow your way smoothly. This is the way the world works. There is a higher power bathing us with abundant light, offering us health and prosperity. You just need to have faith, but not blind faith. Trust God, as well as your own powers and the power of Physics to guide you on your path.

3

THE SHORTCUT TO BYPASS NEGATIVE ENERGETIC INFLUENCES AND AWAKEN SPIRITUALLY

The present moment is just as important as the next. If you are always thinking about the future and what it is going to bring in your life, you are always lacking things. You do not embrace the moment, visualizing what is about to come your way. The truth is, what you are looking for never actually arrives. You always want more, which is exhausting and keeps you in a state of need. Instead of fully appreciating what is going on in your life at the present moment, you are wasting your time thinking about "What if..." and you are not enjoying your life to its fullest potential.

People often live their life focused on an end destination. They spend their days fantasizing about a specific place, a particular moment in the future where they have accomplished their goals. They try to picture themselves getting a promotion, walking down the aisle to say "I do" to their significant other, losing those extra pounds that have been making them sad, finally going out with that handsome guy they met at the gym. The list goes on and on, leaving plenty of room for those fantasies.

Of course, there is nothing wrong with dreaming big. In fact, this is the only way for us to accomplish things. We set a goal and do whatever it takes to achieve that goal in a timely, satisfying

SPIRITUAL GROWTH FOR WOMEN

manner. However, in the process, we must never neglect the present moment. Walking towards a destination is just as important as reaching that destination, although many would argue with that. If we undervalue the present moment, then we tend to live on a dream rather than face reality and its pure beauty.

There will always be mental projections of new goals, as soon as you have successfully conquered your current ones. Unless you learn how to appreciate every moment, you will never stop living in the thought. Rather than enjoying what each moment brings, you will constantly be thinking of your next accomplishment. Even if this comes your way, it will only offer you a brief moment of satisfaction. Soon after, you realize there is another thing that deserves your fullest attention and it is again set in the future.

What you continuously overlook is that all these moments you neglect to appreciate make up the vast percentage of your life. By focusing solely on the future, you give up so many wonderful things. You waste your time absorbed in your thoughts when you could be enjoying every minute and appreciate its uniqueness. Every breath you take is a blessing. How can you be at peace with all the thoughts about the future spoiling your mood, making you feel on edge? You need to let go of this constant yearning for more and just be present.

Imagine all the little objects you use every day. I am sure you consider most of them as a means to an end. You pick up a glass of water and you drink without thinking twice about it. You use the laptop to check your emails, you cook in the same pot and you cannot even recall its exact color. Even though these objects are partly a means to an end, they are able to bring some temporary enjoyment to your life. By looking at them, feeling them, giving them your full attention without any interference from your thoughts, you will surely discover new aspects of these items.

Through this process of becoming fully aware, you will be able to bypass negative thoughts and avoid self-sabotage. You will have the power to enhance your immune system, fighting off several

ANGELA GRACE

ailments that derive from a lack of balance within your body. It all starts there, deep inside you. As soon as you learn how to connect to the world around you and simply be, you will notice a huge difference in your life.

LET GO OF YOUR EGO

Take a moment and picture a rock star getting on stage, with thousands of people singing along and shouting their name. They feel their ego skyrocket and they love it. As they are not self-aware, they rely on other people to define themselves. They feel powerful and important, enjoying the moment when their dreams and fantasies have finally been made true. After the concert, though, they go backstage and in the end, they return home. This is when reality hits them hard. There is a sense of insufficiency that brings them down and this explains why substance abuse is so common for them. They cannot handle that huge shift in their life.

Coming to terms with your reality is of the essence in your path towards self-awareness. You must embrace all aspects of your life and not hold anything back. Even those traits you deem as negative are part of who you are. By acknowledging that they exist, you immediately hold yourself accountable for your actions. This is amazing, as it triggers your self-growth. Unless you are able to look right through you, you cannot expect to thrive in life and improve yourself.

Most people tend to overlook those aspects of their personality they wish they didn't have. For instance, a person might be overly shy. They will tend to neglect that part when thinking about themselves. This makes no sense, as you will still be shy. You will just not talk about it, choosing to forget and ultimately creating a false image about yourself. However, such a false image is only short-lived. You cannot go on with your life neglecting a trait of yours. Sooner or later, it will come to the surface. It is best that you are prepared for that moment.

SPIRITUAL GROWTH FOR WOMEN

From the moment you realize that there are certain parts about your life you would rather not have, a whole new world of possibilities unfolds before you. Now you have the power to change those traits, as long as you are aware of their existence. If you envy others for their accomplishments, you need to work on that and figure out where this characteristic stems from. Over time, you will see that it will fade away and not bother you as much. The same goes for various other elements of your personality, even though there will always be parts that you do not quite like.

It is crucial that you understand you are imperfect. All humans are imperfect and this is absolutely fine. You are bound to make mistakes as others do. In the end, you are only human and mistakes are part of your learning process. At the same time, it is important to comprehend that you are not a better person than others in the world. We have been raised to believe that we are special. This is partly true. We are special, but so is everyone else around us. Every person is unique, amazing, and filled with infinite possibilities.

As a result, you let go of your ego and you focus on the bigger picture. You recognize your ego and disassociate from it so that you can move on and progress. Unless you do that, you will be limited to your own perception of the world. This is just a tiny portion of the universe and you should get rid of the anchors you have set yourself. Instead, you should concentrate on how to expand, rather than contract in your life. Self-awareness will help you achieve that, broadening your horizons and allowing you to reach enlightenment.

Exercises for Living in the Present

How can you live in the present? You cannot expect to master this art from one moment to the next. On the contrary, it takes time and dedication for you to be able to reject all other thoughts and just be present. Over time, it gets easier, and eventually, it flows naturally from within. If you are determined to live in the present moment, though, you need to practice through the use of several thoughts, affirmations, mantras, and more. In this way, you will get the opportunity to influence emotions, changing how you feel about yourself.

One great thing to do is go out and get closer to nature. While you are doing that, try to observe every little detail. Watch the flowers with the morning dew, see the bees flying over them in anticipation of enjoying their pollen. See the tree leaves gently moving back and forth, following the breeze that is also fondling your cheeks and messing with your hair. Smell all those aromas from the flowers and the wet soil. Listen to the birds chirping, the animals trying to communicate in a language that is unknown, yet greatly fascinating to you.

As you are looking more closely, you become more aware of both yourself and your surroundings. Listen to the sounds of your steps, as you are walking down the path. Notice how you are feeling, how you are perceiving all those external stimulants. Feel the sun warming you with its generous sunlight, illuminating all things around you. Get rid of any other thoughts that might be trying to creep into your mind. This is the beauty of the world calling out to you. Do not spoil the moment with anything else other than your present reality. Soon, you will realize how much you have been missing out on all this time.

Otherwise, you can easily do a similar exercise at home. You can practice sitting and living in presence by eliminating all thoughts. Just focus on a single item within the room. Try to elaborate on its details. Its shape, color, texture, size—all these characteristics make it exactly the way it is. Notice how this item makes you feel. Do not distract yourself with anything else than this object. This will help

SPIRITUAL GROWTH FOR WOMEN

you gain perspective of reality, away from the distorting lenses you have been using so far.

By doing so, you realize what the surface reality looks like. You get to see its beauty, perceiving things through your sensory system and without any interference from your thought patterns. Along with this beauty, you also have the chance to perceive an underlying sense of stillness. You are still and present. So you learn how to distinguish two different levels of presence. Imagine you are talking to someone. You should be focusing on the words coming out of your mouth and perceive the surface reality including the person you are talking to, the place you are located, and so on.

At the same time, you should be able to comprehend where these words originate. Many people would claim that words originate from the mind. Nevertheless, this is not true. The mind actually helps by formulating those words. If you pay attention, though, you will see that they come from a deeper place within you. This place enables you to experience alert stillness. As the words are formed and you communicate with the person before you, you see the impact these words have on your body and mind.

Another great way for you to remain grounded and connected to the world is to start your day with a mindful body scan. Focus on each part of your body, repeating affirmations about it. In this way, you let your mind know that you are fully aware of yourself. Start from the head and finish with the toes, always practicing deep breathing. You can also use EFT tapping while you are recognizing the parts of your body. Alternatively, you are free to engage in morning meditation. Just close your eyes and think of your breathing. Relax with every breath you inhale and exhale, focusing on nothing else but this moment.

Of course, being present in the moment could not be complete without journaling. You can dedicate a few minutes every morning, writing down everything that comes to mind. Let your thoughts flow naturally and do not worry about grammar or typos. Write about your plans for the day, the goals you have set for the foresee-

ANGELA GRACE

able future, your feelings, and your dreams. By doing that, you can visualize the things you wish to achieve in life. Finally, express your gratitude through this process. Give thanks to the world for all your blessings. They are more than what you would have imagined and it is great to see them on paper, as a point of reference.

If you love yoga, then a salutation to the sun is an excellent way to live in the present moment. Sun salutations have been tradition-ally used for thousands of years to usher in the new day. You can do them in the morning or literally every time of the day you feel like it. What you need are some comfortable clothes and a yoga mat. Stand upright with your feet slightly apart. Then move your shoul-ders up and down, opening the chest, while lifting your toes and putting all your weight on your heels. Bring your arms over your head. Stay like this for a few moments and then take your arms and move them in front of your body and downwards, until you touch your toes. If you are not used to yoga, you may need to bend your knees slightly to achieve this pose painlessly.

Breathe deeply and allow your head to just hang there, with the crown facing the ground. From that point, you will have to lift your palms and touch your thighs. This will help you expand your torso and back. As soon you feel your spine stretched, resume your previous position with your body folded and your palms touching your toes. Now take the plank pose, with your feet and palms supporting the weight of your body. Lift your hips, so that you engage the core and balance your body properly. You will feel your energy flowing from your heels.

After a few moments, lower your body and release your feet. You will need to lie down, keeping your palms on the ground. Following that, you will have to lift your torso and get the cobra pose. Now, lift your hips and touch the ground with your feet again. This is the dog facing downwards pose in yoga. Your body will seem as if it has created a triangle. Take some baby steps, so that your feet get closer to your arms and you resume your initial folding pose. Lift your palms until they touch your thighs again and repeat the same process, folding down your body once more and then moving your arms all the way up on top of your head. By now, you will be standing upright and you will be breathing deeply. Finally, get your arms to your heart center and keep those palms connected to each other, just like you are praying.

❧ 4 ❧

LOOK AT YOUR LIFE AND BE HONEST.... ARE YOU READY TO LET GO OF WHAT NO LONGER SERVES YOU?

Have you ever found yourself trapped in a toxic relationship? Have you ever wondered why you have to put up with all this hurtful stuff in your life? I am sure you have found plenty of examples to share. There are many people out there eager to suck on your energy and bring you down. They can be family members and loved ones, friends and mere acquaintances, colleagues, and associates. Everyone within your social environment can make it to the list. This is the list of people you should stay away from if you are determined to reach your higher self and find your true calling in life.

Relationships can be hard. I know that all too well. You grow up surrounded by people and you do not even question their motives. In fact, you take it for granted that those around you are there to protect you. However, reality is much different. Ever since you are little and you are powerless to react, you shape your beliefs based on what your family teaches you. You get to learn by following in the footsteps of grown-ups and peers. This is why people within a family develop similar personality traits. It is the daily interaction with each other that makes it easier to behave in a similar manner.

As you grow older, more social groups come into your life. Obvi-

SPIRITUAL GROWTH FOR WOMEN

ously, your family continues playing an important role in your upbringing and sets the ground rules of your everyday life. There are also educational institutions like school, sports clubs, organizations, and other opportunities for you to enhance your social life and get out there into the real world. Their power over you is just as haunting as that of your family. You are struggling to fit in, sometimes at the expense of your own personality. At times, you find yourself pretending to be someone you are not. You only do that to be accepted by those you value the most.

Going against the dominant thinking of these groups is extremely hard. To some, it might even seem impossible. You feel compelled to follow the norm and this typically involves going with the flow. Still, this can be the only way to feel good about yourself. Humans are meant to form groups and be together. They are not supposed to live in isolation. This is true, but the groups that are formed should not be based on inequality. On the contrary, they need to be created in a way that promotes prosperity for all.

You should not be made the victim. If you suspect that somebody is trying to do that, it is time to walk away. Stand up for yourself and for your beliefs. Do not compromise, just because you wish to continue being in the same group. It is not worth it, as this compromise is going to eat you up from inside. You will be constantly feeling inferior to others since this is what others have made you feel. They have projected all these negative beliefs to you and you have been convinced that they are true. Well, they are not.

All these toxic personalities have come to gain control over you. They have enslaved you and you feel trapped. Even if there are moments of clarity when you realize what is going on, it seems that you cannot escape. You are drawn into their misery and you feel miserable too. Although you might believe you are not worthy of something more, you are. Nobody should treat you like that, taking advantage of you or making fun of you. If they cannot appreciate what you have to offer, then you should not be around them.

What you need to do is be surrounded by positive people. They will lift you up and show you the way your life should be. Through their positive energy, they will elevate your own vibrational frequency. As a result, you will be able to attract more wonderful things into your life. If you are surrounded by toxic people, negative energy overwhelms you and you are unable to claim what is yours. You cannot help but fall deeper into this dark pit, where you see nothing else but a shadow of who you really are.

I am not saying that you should reject all past relationships. The bonds of family and life-long friends are very powerful. Perhaps you can let those people into your life, assuming they fit the profile of the people you want to associate with. Ask yourself the following questions and you will realize what you have to do: Do they accept me for who I am? Do they support me, no matter what? Do they love me unconditionally and without any hidden agenda? Do I feel good when I am around them?

Be honest with your answers, as they will determine your future with these people. Even though it may be painful, it is essential that you cut the cord of toxic relationships. What's the point in remaining trapped in a relationship that offers you nothing, whereas you are expected to give and give all the time? Why would you ever put yourself second? You need to love and cherish yourself, making your own well-being a top priority. Whoever wishes to help you achieve that is more than welcome to join you. All others are free to leave and not look back. Your door will be closed from now on to toxic people and those who think ill of you.

Don't think that I am asking you to become selfish. It is not selfish to look out for yourself. If you don't do that, no one else ever will. You have come here to live your life to its fullest potential, accomplishing great things while staying true to your higher calling. Your purpose is divine and nothing should stand in the way, preventing you from achieving your goal. Believe in yourself and don't let others convince you that you are anything short of awesome.

CLEAR YOUR AURA FROM NEGATIVITY

Aura is the subtle manifestation of who you are. By taking a look at a person's aura, you can see plenty of things about themselves. You can see if they are healthy or if they are suffering from any disease. In addition, you are able to notice several aspects of their mental health and emotional well-being. If you want to feel better, you immediately focus on how to cleanse your aura. In case there are energy blocks, they will show in your aura and they will hinder your progress. Of course, your aura is not independent of other people's vibrational frequencies.

When you are close to another person, you connect with them on a deep level. A bond is created between your energetic field and theirs, establishing cords that bring both of you closer together. These cords are not necessarily bad. When there is mutual love, respect, appreciation, or other positive feelings manifested between the two individuals, the cords are vessels that transfer these amazing emotions and elevate both your vibrational frequencies. Otherwise, the same cords can be toxic and you need to clear your aura from all negativity.

If you want to purify your body and spirit, you can use guided meditation to clear your aura from negative thought patterns. Negative energy is concentrated on the first three energetic centers or chakras of your body, from the solar plexus down. Root chakra carries the stagnant energy that has been created from mistrust and fear. Old feelings of rage, guilt, shame, and anger are stuck in the sacral chakra. Finally, issues that are related to self-esteem or the ability to move forward in life lead to energy discrepancies in the third, solar plexus chakra. In these first three chakras, there is a wealth of information as to past experiences from childhood to your current state in life.

Although you cannot actually change the past and what has been done in your life, you can transmute these past memories and experiences. As a result, you will feel relieved from the burden of having

ANGELA GRACE

to endure negative energy within your body. Depending on your wounds from the past, take deep breaths and concentrate on the respective energy center where such imbalance stems from. In this way, you will be able to reclaim that part of your body and take control of its energy.

Assuming you are holding on to feelings of guilt, focus your breathing towards your sacral chakra. Feel the air upon inhaling. Direct your breath to your abdominal area and let it flow smoothly, getting rid of any stagnant energy that has accumulated over the years. If you feel that resistance is intense, then you should consider staying there a little longer and repeating your breathing cleanse. All these negative emotions that have been suppressed will eventually leave your body if you concentrate on this ritual.

It is best if you start with the root chakra and move all the way up to your solar plexus, breathing in and exhaling these negative feelings. After having completed this process, you can lean backward and connect to your pillar of light. Visualize this bright light shining down to you from the divine source. Open your chakras and let the light shine through, cleansing the energy and leaving you rejuvenated.

This offers you abundant support so that you can get past these distractions and get back on your path towards self-growth. Let your energy centers expand with light. The entire process enables you to become grounded and allows your body to align fully with the universe. Instead of thinking with your mind, your focus is now in your heart chakra. Any negative vibration from your body will eventually go away, bringing divine light into every single cell of yours.

Besides opening your energy centers, there are several other things you can do to clear your aura from negativity. First of all, you can take a shower. The power of water running down on you is hugely therapeutic. You purify your skin and get rid of any dirt, while at the same time disposing yourself of energy blocks. Take a moment and think of the times you were feeling sad or frustrated.

SPIRITUAL GROWTH FOR WOMEN

You got into the shower and soon after you felt that all your troubles have washed away. This is not just in your mind. Water is cleansing and you can benefit from its amazing energy.

On top of that, you can also try mudding. By doing so, you will get the opportunity to feel absolutely grounded and connected to the universe. Mud stimulates purification and helps you stabilize your energy levels. If you want to take it a step further, you are free to try out neem leaves. Their properties are extremely helpful and they allow your aura to be thoroughly cleansed. In addition, you can burn sage and purify your energy centers through the smoke. You will see that any stagnant energy gets removed and you amplify your vibration. Last but not least, go out in the open air and feel the gentle breeze running through your body.

Walk Away When It's Time

I am sure you have identified yourself as a part of at least a toxic relationship. If you have, I sincerely hope that you were able to cut the cord and let yourself free of their negativity. Otherwise, you are strongly advised to do so as soon as possible. There are many reasons keeping you from actualizing that decision to get rid of whatever no longer serves your purpose. I am well aware of that. You might have lived your entire life with them or you may have exchanged vows of eternal love and devotion. You might think you cannot make it on your own, whether on a personal or on a professional level.

There is ground to these doubts. I am not advising you to let go of the past and forget everything that has happened in your life so far. This cannot happen and there is no need for you to let go of your memories. These are the ones that have formed your current reality. They have forged your personality, making you stronger and more confident. They are part of your world and yourself. However, no excuse should prolong this misery of being tangled into a toxic relationship.

I am not advising you against giving people second chances. Forgiveness is a virtue. Rather than holding grudges and poisoning your mind with negative thoughts, you should be able to let go and start fresh. There are moments when people come to you in regret and they ask for you to forgive them. If their regret is sincere, then you need to consider this option. Nevertheless, this can be part of their attempt to manipulate you. Despite what you may think, there are narcissists out there and people who will do anything to cloud your judgment.

Although each case is unique, there are several signs you should consider red flags. As soon as you spot these red flags, you need to stay away. Distance yourself from these people, since they will most likely harm you in the long run. Always remember that you are destined for great things and you must have the right people beside you. So even if your heart is torn and you are fighting off the urge to forgive others, there are cases you had better walk away from. If you don't, you will be dragged into negative incidents and you will be tormented. You don't deserve that.

First of all, you owe no loyalty to abusive people. Whenever there is abuse of any sort, you must go away and never look back. It doesn't matter how long you know the abuser. They jeopardize your path towards self-awareness and spiritual growth. When you get involved in a relationship with a master manipulator like that, you will see that they are trying to lure you in and then fill you with guilt. Instead of lifting your spirit and making you feel good about yourself, they will point the finger at you and blame you for everything.

SPIRITUAL GROWTH FOR WOMEN

It is not rare for individuals to make up excuses, just to validate other people's injustice to them. They convince themselves that they have misinterpreted their behavior or they have made a huge mistake, leading to that outburst of hostility, aggression, and humiliation against them. In many cases, you will try to make excuses to justify the way an abuser behaves to you. There is no excuse whatsoever, no matter what you have done wrong. Nothing justifies abuse. Verbally or physically abusive people do not deserve such a thought process. Build a support network and get away from those toxic, abusive relationships.

I am not saying you should be firm and straightforward or avoiding listening to the other side of the story. When you sit down calmly and discuss with another person, you often realize that your way of looking at things is not the only one. It is essential that you figure out a way to connect with others on a deeper level and honest communication is key. Don't bail on everyone, but instead open up dialogue and have a meaningful conversation about your requests. If the person next to you is unwilling to sit down and talk about the things that have been troubling you, then this relationship will be short-lived.

Moving forward with the people you should not waste any more time with, there are those who neglect you and your needs repeatedly. Your loved ones need to take care of you, just like you take care of them. Every person needs respect and compassion in their life. If you notice that you do not receive what you deserve from your relationship, then it is time to confront them and make your requests. Should that behavioral pattern persist, it is time to let go. There is no reason for you to lower your expectations or give without taking anything back in return. In fact, respect and appreciation should be given to you generously and without even having to point it out or ask.

Repeated lies should also tip you off about having to move on with your life. A relationship should be based on honesty. Otherwise, how can you establish trust? If you have repeatedly found out

33

that the person next to you is lying, you know what you have to do. They have promised to quit that lying, they have committed to change, but they keep on doing the same things over and over. This is hurtful and you do not deserve such treatment. The best thing you can do for a liar is to cut them free. At that point in their life, they have no intention of quitting that harmful habit and you cannot put yourself in such a negative situation.

Obviously, maybe this is a wake-up call for them to realize that their actions come with tangible reactions and the repercussions are severe. If you are afraid that you will not find another person like that, you will be surprised by how many amazing and honest people are out there. They are eager to offer you exactly what you want in life, including support and generosity, empathy, and real concern. Unlike what you might believe, the vast majority of people do not fit the profile of narcissists and sociopaths. So don't settle for one of those.

You should not stay in a relationship that takes you for granted and shows no appreciation for what you do. Showing respect is of paramount importance, as it reveals the true intentions of the people around you. Maybe you have been working hard at the office but no one gives you credit. Perhaps you have been taking care of your loved ones and still, they do not even recognize your efforts. No matter the situation, you should not diminish your expectations. Instead, you should demand what you are entitled to and never lower your dreams.

Never forget that you cannot have a positive life with a negative mindset. Get rid of those people around you who do not serve your true calling anymore. Thank them for all the time they have spent around you, as everyone has given something new to you. Everyone has contributed towards reaching your current self. Be grateful for your experiences with them, but don't make any excuses to prolong the inevitable. Cut the cord and be on your way to skyrocket your self-growth!

DIVINE FEMININE ENERGY AND HOW TO STOP CARING WHAT OTHER PEOPLE THINK OF YOU

Humans have been blessed with a feminine and a masculine side, which complement one another. It feels like yin and yang, as an archetypal concept of dualism that is omnipresent in the world. The masculine energy has been associated with logic and practical activities. On the other hand, feminine energy is all about creativity, intuition, and emotions. Obviously, each person should embrace both these aspects of their existence. No one can only survive on logic or listening to their feelings. However, in modern society, there is clear discrimination against feminine energy.

Most women grow up believing that showing their feminine side actually reveals weakness. This could not be further from the truth. It takes courage to feel empathy and compassion, as much as creating and trusting your inner self. What would logic mean without love or creativity? Feminine power is overwhelming, as long as you know how to reach it and fully comprehend its essence. By tapping into your feminine divine power, basically, you wake up the core of who you really are. The results are purely mesmerizing.

Yet, this power remains dormant until you consciously decide to set it on fire. This is the moment when you realize everything you

ANGELA GRACE

have thought was true is only making you weaker. Rather than settling for life, you have been programmed by others to live, you can strengthen your spiritual growth by awakening your divine feminine energy. I have written a book on this particular subject, called *Feminine Energy Awakening* and you are more than welcome to discover your true higher self with a little of my personal guidance and help.

As mentioned earlier in this book, water is a powerful cleansing element. It also holds a wealth of information. So if you are determined to awaken your divine feminine energy, you need to indulge in bath time rituals. In this way, every time you take a bath you can let go of your old self and engage in a rebirth. Fill your bathtub with warm lukewarm water and add your favorite essential oils. You can use chamomile, myrrh, cypress, lavender, orange or lemon. Around 15 drops are perfect. Add some dead sea salt as it contains more minerals than normal sea salt. Dip into the water and use a scrub to exfoliate and purify your skin.

Apart from that, you can listen to music that elevates your vibrational frequencies. Depending on your mood, you are free to experiment with different types of music that appeal to you. Above anything else, however, you need to take the time and dedicate yourself to this awakening process. Listen to yourself and feel your energy. Everything is vibration and therefore you should devote time and effort to this endeavor.

In order to tap into your divine feminine energy, you should embrace your ability to create. Any form of art will help you to express your inner thoughts and fantasies, by creating something that speaks right to your heart. Collaborate with other women, so that you work collectively and join forces in your journey towards self-actualization. You can attend "women only" groups, where you discuss what womanhood means to you. Don't get me wrong; I love men and I respect them. However, sometimes it can be hard for a woman to open up about their emotions and struggles in the presence of a man.

SPIRITUAL GROWTH FOR WOMEN

Furthermore, it is great if you can explore your sensuality. Celebrate the beauty in your life and surround yourself with an aesthetically pleasing environment. Indulge in simple everyday pleasures that make you feel great about yourself. Take a long salt bath and listen to your favorite music. Explore your sexuality, as your body should never be off-limits to you. Instead, you ought to know how to get sexual pleasure and therefore delve into the magic of sexuality. In this way, you will also have the chance to release hormones that promote satisfaction and wholeness.

Another aspect of your life that is directly linked to your divine feminine energy is your mindset towards being a woman and a mother. Therefore, prior to discovering this immense power within yourself, you should first analyze what you think of these concepts. What does being a woman mean to you? Does it mean being powerless or independent and strong? Does being a woman make you unable to take charge of things, always relying on a man to provide? These questions will shed light on your own mentality and they will help you understand how you feel about femininity.

Every woman is unique and so there is not a single right answer to these questions. Instead, you must explore your own truth and see where your beliefs stem from. For instance, you might think that being a woman comes with a lack of acting sensibly. Why do you believe that? Is it because your family has raised you this way? Maybe the women you have turned to as role models behaved irrational, never taking logic into consideration. Or perhaps the men in your environment have always blamed women for doing so. Find the real reasons behind those limiting beliefs of yours and turn them over to your advantage.

When it comes to motherhood, again it doesn't matter if you are planning to have a baby or not. It doesn't matter if you ever want to experience that aspect of femininity. What matters is your attitude. What do you feel about motherhood? Is this something intimidating or off-putting for you? Does it make you want to run away or do you consider it the ultimate life purpose? Maybe your attitude has been affected by your own mother. What's your relationship with her? You need to let go of any anger or resentment. Instead, you should forgive her for any past mistakes. Even if you do not restore your relationship, you need to be able and forgive to move forward.

Overall, divine feminine essence is who you really are and what you should be manifesting in life. Once you have discovered its infinite power, your life will be totally transformed. You will celebrate your femininity in the most extraordinary manner, completing your true calling in life and feeling great about it. As soon as you dispose of any negative thoughts poisoning your life, you will be able to see clearly and find your place in the world. Fully aligned with the universe, connected to this primitive and overwhelming power, you will finally enjoy life exactly the way you deserve.

STOP CARING ABOUT WHAT OTHER PEOPLE THINK OF YOU

Have you ever paused for a moment, thinking about the significance of other people's opinions in your life? Why does that matter to you so much? Although people learn to value what others say about them, this can lead to a slippery slope. You get to depend on external factors, rather than focus on your very own powers. Remember that your self-confidence is one of your major assets. You can only grow spiritually by letting go of caring what other people think of you.

Do you invest too much value into what others think or say

SPIRITUAL GROWTH FOR WOMEN

about you, no matter if they are really close to you or they are complete strangers? If you do so, you let others define you. Are you sure you want to do that? Take a moment and think about a reality where you didn't care about what others thought of you. What would happen then? There are endless possibilities unfolding before your eyes since you would be able to decide on your own without any interference from third parties. No matter what you did, you would be happier and lighter in your life.

I understand that people are usually plagued by their own insecurities. Yet, most of the time these insecurities hold no real ground. In fact, in a hectic everyday life, most people do not even care about your actions. You tend to overanalyze things and be a harsh critic of your behavior. Others do not see it like that and so you need to start looking at your life from a different perspective. They are too consumed in their own worries and challenges, just like you. Don't feel like all eyes are on you. More often than not, they fret over the same things as you, so you are all in this together.

Why would you continue living by the narrative of other people? By valuing someone else's opinion over yours, you immediately sabotage yourself and your life-long goals. What should matter is your own opinion, as you know all the parameters and you are fully aware of your current standing. You should determine who you want to be and commit to becoming that person, no matter what others think. On the contrary, when you neglect your personal views to conform with your peers and those around you, what you do is hand them over your power. Why would you ever give up on the control you possess over your life?

Sometimes caring about what others think of you reveals an underlying strive for perfection. Do you feel compelled to pursue a flawless performance in every single thing you do, even though you know this is fruitless? By taking on such impossible endeavors, you are bound to damage your self-esteem and confidence. You may even operate based on the subconscious perceptions you have developed about yourself since childhood. In order to get past this horrible conundrum, you should focus on self-acceptance. Accept yourself and who you really are, setting realistic goals, and feeling happy.

One more thing you can do to enjoy life more and not worry over other people's opinions is just not care. Even though it might seem simplistic at first, it is in fact the best way to deal with things that tend to take control over your mind. Be selective about what you value in life. You cannot be expected to care about every single thing, can you? This can be catastrophic, as it will lead to endless moments of emotional distress. Instead, pick your battles and set your priorities straight.

The next challenge is a really hard one, but it will shift your mindset more than you would possibly have imagined. Once you accept that not everyone likes you, your life becomes so much easier. I am sure you want others to think highly of you. Their approval means a lot, as they validate who you are and this is a great way to boost your ego. However, you cannot be pleasant to everyone. Depending on their personality, their place in the world, and their current struggles, they might or might not find you likable. This is perfectly understandable and it frankly has nothing to do with you—it is on them.

Based on everything that has been pointed out above, do you think you can stop caring about what other people think of you? This is the only way for you to take on the challenges that come along in your life. Otherwise, you will always look back and think twice, afraid that someone judges you harshly. You need to be aware that making mistakes is inevitable. It is life's method of teaching us all the valuable lessons we need to acquire. Don't underestimate their value and do not shy away from the challenge. As soon as you surpass your fear of failing and making mistakes, nothing will be able to stop you from achieving greatness.

Exercises to Awaken Your Divine Feminine Energy

There are many techniques that allow you to awaken your divine feminine energy. First of all, you can use positive affirmations to

SPIRITUAL GROWTH FOR WOMEN

project what you wish to accomplish in life and manifest it, based on the principles of the Law of Attraction. Start your day by spending a few minutes focusing on your blessings. Embrace your feminine power and enhance your potential. You can use the following affirmations, picking the ones that truly make your heart glow:

- I am worthy.
- I am safe.
- I am filled with light.
- I am abundant.
- My life is filled with love and compassion.
- I have a beautiful loving heart.
- I am deeply connected to my divine feminine energy.
- Being a woman makes my heart open.
- I love and accept myself completely and unconditionally.
- I am in touch with my creativity.
- I embrace my own divine nature.
- I am beautiful inside and outside.
- I am wise and intuitive.
- I am compassionate.
- The universe guides me in my life.
- I trust myself.
- I radiate love and harmony.
- I am receptive.
- I am humble and confident.
- The relationships I build with others are based on love and understanding.

By repeating those wonderful affirmations about yourself, you lay the foundations of awakening your spirituality. You will feel energized, as these amazing words amplify your vibrational frequency and make you feel happier. You can also try journaling. Instead of visualizing your divine feminine energy, you are free to

41

depict these thoughts on paper. Write down what your inner goddess dictates. How are you feeling? What emotions does this awakening spark? Refer to those scripts every time you want extra motivation, so as to stay true to your journey towards self-growth.

Another great technique used to awaken your divine feminine energy is meditation. Sit down comfortably and close your eyes. Concentrate on your breathing. Inhale through the nose for 4 seconds, before you exhale through the mouth for 5 seconds. Repeat that breathing sequence a few times, until you feel completely relaxed. Bring awareness to your body, breathing gently. Let go of any tension and concentrate on your heart beating. Visualize a red light emerging from the depths of the earth and filling your body through your feet and upwards. While you are doing that, you can chant a mantra to make this meditation even more powerful. Chant a mantra that awakens the cosmic forces and connects you to your inner goddess, such as the following: *"Maha Shakti Namah Shri."* Let go of the image and slowly bring your awareness to your surroundings.

Another exceptional method used widely to heal your energy and restore any traumas is EFT tapping. Through this powerful and highly flexible tool, you can accomplish amazing things in life. Below, I am going to show you how to use EFT tapping to stop caring about what other people say about you. You need to concentrate on your meridian points, which are specific parts of your body where energy is accumulated. By using your fingers, you start tapping on the exterior of your palm and then move on to the top of your head, your third eye chakra right between your eyebrows, your cheekbones, upper lip, and chin. Next, you go even further down to your neck and either side of your neckline, your chest, your heart, and under your armpits.

While you are tapping these different parts of your body, you should repeat the following: *"Even though I care about what other people think about me, I choose to love and accept myself. Although I worry about what others say about me, I choose to love and honor myself. If I allow*

SPIRITUAL GROWTH FOR WOMEN

myself to do what I want to do, other people will think horrible things about me. This doesn't feel safe. However, I still love, accept, and honor myself completely. I worry about what other people think of me, what they say, and what they do and so I hold myself back and deprive myself of things. I do that for fear of what others might think. I am surrendering my power to other people and I choose to stop that. I am clearing this fear out, releasing it all the way back through my past. All these times in the past, I have assumed that others would say bad things about me. Even though I am afraid, I choose to trust my higher self. As I clear this fear from my life, I remove those people who have been thinking badly of me. I don't want them in my life. I choose to do great things in my life, as I love and accept myself for who I am."

❦ 6 ❧

CORD CUTTING, RELEASING SPIRITUAL BLOCKS, THE BEAUTY OF FORGIVENESS AND SPIRITUAL CLEANSING

Being trapped in relationships that no longer serve your life purpose can be toxic. It distracts you from your path towards enlightenment and self-growth, blocking your spirituality and keeping you trapped in a vicious cycle of negativity. If you realize that those around you are not entangled in your energy, then you need to cut the cord and let go of them. Cord-cutting is a symbolic reference to the miracle of birth, where the baby is separated from the mother with an abrupt cutting of the cord. Even though this is a huge shock for the baby, it actually allows for exponential growth in the real world.

Just like the baby, you should be looking forward to your disconnection from negative people that have nothing to offer you. I know they might be your life-long friends and companions, your relatives, and those you cannot imagine living without. Still, why do you want them around? Have they ever been useful, making you feel good or helping you achieve something great? Of course, I am not saying you should get rid of all the people in your life. On the contrary, having a great supportive network can help you a great deal in your journey towards self-growth. However, negativity does not serve your needs. It poisons you from within.

SPIRITUAL GROWTH FOR WOMEN

There are many people out there who are eager to feed on your energy. They exhaust you as they are constantly demanding from you to give them your fullest attention. You always give and give, even though nothing seems to be enough. They are insatiable. When they realize that you are no longer able to provide them with the energy they need, they most likely leave in pursuit of someone who caters to these needs. Rather than establishing healthy and meaningful relationships, they are more concerned about their personal gain and agenda than anything else.

You may have been trapped in such relationships for years and years on end. You might have identified them as difficult people, energy vampires, narcissists, and bad energy people. Yet, you are still lingering and you feel unable to move on in your life. In fact, at times it feels as if you have created a codependent relationship. If this is the case, you should take charge of your life and finally do what you have to. Unless you get rid of these negative interferences, you cannot anticipate all the wonderful things associated with spiritual self-growth. Instead, you will keep on feeding those people's negativity and eventually get drowned in an ocean of despair.

What you need to comprehend is that it is none of your business to save someone who doesn't want to be saved. If you have been dragged in such a behavioral pattern where you continuously help others in need, take a step back. Do they deserve your attention? Are they worthy of what you are offering to them? If they are not, then you shouldn't be around them. You need to evaluate your relationship based on tangible evidence, rather than your feelings. Be careful, as oftentimes these people tend to be manipulative and trigger feelings of guilt. This is how they lure others and bend them according to their will.

Set healthy boundaries to withstand the pressure they might be putting on you to offer more. There are intrusive people who do not care about you and so they knock on your door every single time they want something. They have no respect for you and they value nothing else but their own needs. Should you encounter such a

45

ANGELA GRACE

person, be sure to build a defensive mechanism that allows you to distance yourself from their presence. Otherwise, you will be sucked into a vortex and it will be difficult to get out.

There will be times when you are doubting yourself and the decision of yours to cut these people out of your life. Don't fall into this trap, as you need to reclaim your energy and get back on the right track towards success. Repeat affirmations about your relationship, so that you remember what you should opt for, instead of settling for endless repetition of misery and negativity. You are entitled to so much more and these people surrounding you will only hinder your progress.

After having dealt with the toxic people in your life, it is only fair that you remove any toxicity from within your body and spirit. Focus on your energetic fields and maintain them free from any blockages. Maintain an elevated vibrational frequency, which will allow you to manifest every single thing you have ever wanted in your life. It is all about Quantum Physics and the Law of Attraction, driven by your own initiative and your will to grow spiritually.

ALIGNING YOUR CHAKRAS

Chakras represent the seven energy centers within our body, while also having a metaphysical location. They are energetic centers and at the same time, they tie to specific muscles, tendons, and nerves in those regions. When you are feeling negative emotions such as anxiety, anger, or fear, this will cause an imbalance in those chakras. As a result, your energy levels drop dramatically and you also manifest physical ailments that stem from that imbalance.

When chakras are cleansed, your aura expands in size and makes you feel wonderful. If there are blockages of accumulated energy that remains stagnant in these centers, your aura shrinks and becomes misshapen. There are pictures that depict those changes, as a form of physical proof that aura does exist ("Aura Photography - How to Read Aura Photos"). This reveals that something is wrong

SPIRITUAL GROWTH FOR WOMEN

and you need to purify your energetic centers across your spine and all the way to the top of your head.

Once you have unlocked and unblocked your chakras, you can have a full Kundalini awakening and this is extremely helpful in your journey to spiritual growth. This will reveal the peak energy level within your body, experiencing an amazing state of consciousness and immense power. You can also attend a reiki/energy healing session to promote thorough unblocking of your energetic fields and feel amazing. Such sessions are available online and it can be a great way to get into contact with like-minded people that share the same interests as you.

You can cleanse your chakras on a daily basis, as soon as you wake up or before going to sleep. Sit comfortably with your spine upright and your legs crossed. Your palms should be on top of your thighs facing the sky. This is a great receiving position, as you will be seeking to receive abundant light from the infinite divine source. Close your eyes and visualize a white light shining down from the sky. The light comes down on you, reaching the top of your head. It flows through you, creating a pillar of light that passes through your crown chakra and then moves towards your third eye chakra.

Feel that light cleansing your energy levels, releasing any stagnant energy that has been holding you back. Experience that lightness, as this energy flows away and you are left with the powerful pure light shining through you. Move further below to your throat chakra and then your heart chakra. Feel its power overwhelming you, cleansing you deeply. Follow the light to your solar plexus chakra, opening your chest and allowing it to flow effortlessly. Move downwards to your sacral chakra and finish with your root chakra, at the base of your spine. Upon completing this cleansing process, visualize the light moving even further below to the ground, reaching the soil and penetrating the earth down to its core.

When you finish this ritual, you will feel lighter and happier. You will have aligned your chakras, keeping them clean and unblocked from any negativity. If you want to take it a step further, you can opt

47

ANGELA GRACE

for the awakening of Kundalini energy. Through the use of the Kundalini sacred chakra dance for women, you can activate that powerful energy and establish a deeper connection to the universe, as well as your divine feminine energy. Again, the focus is drawn to the activation of your chakras.

Start by standing upright and gently spreading your legs, so that you can bend the knees and move your body downwards. You are bending and stretching, moving the root chakra up and down. As you are moving downwards, you spread your arms and move them all the way up to the top of your head. Repeat that ten times, until you feel the energy pumping through the root chakra. To activate your sacral chakra, bend your knees again. This time you visualize your beautiful rose opening up, as you are moving your pelvis right and left in a set rhythm.

Visualize this powerful energy moving upwards to your solar plexus and continue dancing like that. Move your body freely right and left, feeling the energy and moving your arms in front of your chest. Bend your torso a little, so that your face is looking down on the ground and repeat this sequence a few times. For the heart chakra, continue moving your body slowly and focus on the energy flowing right through your heart. Move your shoulders up and down as you are dancing sensually, smiling, and feeling pure bliss overwhelming you. Open the heart by moving each arm above your head and all the way up the sky. As you are moving towards your throat chakra, get that energy flowing and open your shoulders. Take deep breaths and sigh with relief. You can also make sounds, primal sounds without any real meaning. This will activate the vibrations within your throat. Start vibrating your body, starting from your legs and your hips, moving upwards. Shake this energy off from your legs and your palms.

Keep breathing, while keeping one palm before your sacral chakra and one against your heart. Continue dancing gently without worrying about the exact movements of yours. There is no set ritual, as it is crucial for you to maintain the energy flow. Finish the

48

SPIRITUAL GROWTH FOR WOMEN

Kundalini chakra dance with a praying pose. Place both your palms in front of your chest as if you were praying and slowly move these palms all the way up until they reach the top of your head. Breathe deeply and relax. You will feel absolutely refreshed and filled with energy, eager to take on the challenges of life and reaching your fullest potential.

The Power of Forgiveness

People make mistakes and they hurt others in the process. I am sure you have made mistakes in your life. You may have tried to make things right or you may have let things take their course. The fact is that mistakes happen more often than we would like to admit. As a result, we end up hurting innocent people along with hurting ourselves. Unless you truly comprehend that mistakes are part of your identity, you will never come to terms with what they really represent and how they should be resolved. Now picture yourself on the other end of the equation. What happens if you are not the person hurting others, but the person who is wronged by them?

Most likely, you are fierce and strict in your beliefs. You cannot believe how someone could have been so wrong. Sometimes you demand some form of compensation for what you have been put through by the person who has wronged you. You also require an apology as the least that they can do after your ordeal. Of course, it all depends on the severity of the mistake. It is different to confront others after having been given the wrong phone number and after having received the wrong treatment for your ailment. Your wrath is obviously going to vary a great deal, depending on that exact severity.

What you fail to perceive, however, is the fact that mistakes are not always intentional. They might be, but then they are probably called "wrongdoings" or "injustices." Whatever the cause, you should not get into it and try to interpret the situation. If you get an apology, then this is lovely. If not, then nothing has changed for you and your life. Nothing has changed for your path towards spiritual growth. As a consequence, you must think of how this event affects

49

you spiritually and mentally. If you let it take control over your life and awaken all these negative feelings, then you will be affected greatly and you will be bitter, sad, and angry. If you let go, you will continue on your path without any distractions and without any turbulence of your inner peace.

Until you have mastered the art of forgiveness, you have not yet entered the spiritual realm. We are living in a world of imperfect people. Therefore, it is inevitable that we get mistreated more than once in a lifetime. Maybe it is your significant other who has cheated on you, a neighbor who doesn't respect your boundaries, or your mother who has always belittled you. If you don't forgive others, you get filled with resentment. By harboring this terrible sentiment, you fill yourself with toxic waste. In fact, being wronged only holds the power you give to that incident by remembering it.

It is essential that you understand humans come from the material world. That knowledge of nature allows you to see right through the selfish acts of others. As soon as you realize that people only make mistakes and treat you badly because they have drifted away from their higher self, you will stop having high expectations of them. As a result, you will not experience any disappointment in your life due to such terrible behaviors. That's the way the world works. These people will only behave the way they know how—which has nothing to do with you. There is nothing personal and hence you should hold no grudges or seek revenge.

More than that, you need to understand that forgiveness should not be meant as a favor to others. It is actually a favor to yourself, an act of kindness. By not forgiving others, you are poisoning your body and mind. You are affecting your vibrational frequency and you are left feeling even worse than what you felt while being hurt by others. If you want to thrive in life, you must master the virtue of forgiving those who have wronged you unconditionally. Otherwise, you will be stuck in an emotional trigger that prevents you from focusing on what actually matters.

If you are wondering what makes it so difficult to let go of

SPIRITUAL GROWTH FOR WOMEN

resentment and forgive others, the answer lies in our self-centered nature. We need to transform this structure within ourselves, in order to reach those higher levels of self-awareness and spiritual growth. Divine love is a state of eternal forgiveness. If you are determined to receive wonderful things in your life, it is of paramount importance that you project that to the world. You do that by emitting positive energy at the highest possible levels of frequency. If you hold grudges and you live your life pondered in resentment, you cannot achieve that.

Imagine drinking some sort of poison. You drink up and then turn to the person who has wronged you in your life. As you are looking at them, it suddenly hits you. They are not affected by the poison. Instead, you are starting to feel unwell. You are getting dizzy and your heart beats faster. You are sweating and your breath becomes slower. Eventually, you fade out. In the meanwhile, the person who has hurt you remains intact. Maybe they are shocked by what has happened to you, but chances are that they will not lose their sleep over it. So you should always remember that by drinking the poison of resentment, you are only hurting yourself.

Ultimately, forgiveness is a blessing and you should embrace it. Forgive all those people around you who have hurt you, no matter what they have done. Let go of these hurtful memories, heal the wounds, and move forward in your life. This is the best thing you can do for your well-being and your spiritual elevation. Don't get consumed by negativity and do not live in the past. There is nothing there for you to anticipate. More than that, forgive regardless of the other person's intention. Whether or not they have regretted their actions is irrelevant to your forgiveness.

❧ 7 ❧

SPIRITUAL HEALING, CRUSHING DEPRESSION, SETTING BOUNDARIES, AND HOW TO STOP LIVING IN DYSFUNCTION

Take a step back and have a look at your relationships. Starting from early childhood and leading all the way up to your current life, how would you evaluate your relationships with others? Think of the dynamics within your family as you grew up, your significant other and maybe your offspring, your colleagues and associates at work, your life-long friends and mere acquaintances. How would you value those relationships in terms of quality? Do they offer you what you need or do they end up hurting you?

Living in dysfunction can be challenging and those relationships can either contribute to that feeling or help you recover. You need to surround yourself with people who lift your spirit and soothe your soul. People who see the good in you and never question your capabilities, your talents, and ultimately your uniqueness. If you have those people around you, then you deserve one great round of applause. If not, then you need to take a deep breath and get to the root of this problem.

One of the major causes of concern is in fact the lack of healthy boundaries. You might be busy trying to serve the needs of others and you might not realize what impact this has on yourself. There is

SPIRITUAL GROWTH FOR WOMEN

no energy left for you to pursue your daily goals or indulge in self-care. By spending your time being available 24/7, tending to the so-called needs of others, and neglecting yours, you sabotage yourself and prevent your spiritual growth. Therefore, this situation has to change. It is time to take matters into your own hands and think about your life for a change.

Set healthy boundaries, so that others know your availability and the extent of time or energy you are willing to invest in them. For instance, there is always a friend who respects no privacy and calls even in the middle of the night. In fact, they will do that even if there is not an emergency to tackle. They think it is perfectly fine to invade your personal space whenever they feel like it because you have never denied them that privilege. Similarly, a family member might snoop around and always ask you the most indiscreet questions about your personal life. They know you will answer, so they don't think twice about this behavioral pattern.

You must understand that it is good to set healthy boundaries and learn how to say "no" to them. If something doesn't serve your own interests and needs, then you should reject it altogether. Create a list of the things you don't want others to do to you and be honest. Who does that and why have you permitted them to do that so far? Evaluate your relationships and spot any red flags. Then, it is time to state these boundaries. Be straightforward when you announce them to the people around you. Be firm and strict, leaving no room for negotiations. It is highly likely that they are going to make their behavior appear less irritating, just so you might reconsider. They may even try to reason with you or claim that you are being irrational. Don't fall for that trap.

Next time you are confronted with the same behavior, you must prove that you are serious. They will definitely test you so that they can understand how serious your claims are. If all this time you have satisfied all of their requests, it will be difficult for them to accept that this is over. You should maintain the boundaries you have created, in order to let others know you are for real. Otherwise, if you appear to be soft and retreat to their will, they will never stop doing that. They will have seen it with their own eyes that you have a soft spot and your opinion is not solid. You want them to comprehend that you are never going to stand the same behavior and the only way to do that is through your own actions.

Once you learn how to deny others of your fullest attention, you will become as unshakable as a mountain. Nothing will be able to break you. On the contrary, you will feel your self-confidence skyrocket, along with your determination. Others will realize that you are not to be toyed with. In this way, you can see which relationships are meaningful and which are only based on them taking advantage of you. Don't risk drifting away from your goals. You deserve to attract all those wonderful things in your life and you need the right people by your side—all the rest are free to walk away.

BEATING DEPRESSION

Have you been feeling down, wondering if what you are experiencing are symptoms of depression? Even though many people confuse that word and use it in the wrong context, there are in fact several signs pointing out that you are suffering from such a mental ailment. First of all, the feeling of hopelessness is a direct sign that something is wrong. When you feel that you have no actual power over things happening in your life and you cannot find a solution that gets you happy, this can result in depression. You are constantly on the verge of bursting into tears and feel like no one is able to help you out. Another red flag is the lack of pleasure or interest in the things taking place in your everyday life. Maybe you enjoyed hobbies in the past, but now you find no joy or pleasure in them. Essentially, you are feeling that there is no spark in your life anymore.

These are the two major symptoms pointing out to the diagnosis of depression. If you have either of these two symptoms, then there is a high likelihood you are indeed in this emotional vortex and especially if you combine them with other, less severe but equally disturbing, symptoms. Additional signs include sleep issues (insomnia or troubled sleep) and lethargy, drained of energy to do anything other than dragging your body from your bed to the sofa. Even the smallest tasks are exhausting. Another sign is relevant to your appetite. Have you noticed that you cannot eat anything? Has this resulted in dramatic weight loss, even though you have not aimed at that? Or on the contrary, have you found yourself overeating in the middle of the night without even being conscious of what or how much you have consumed?

Similar to that symptom, you might blame yourself for everything and feel like a failure. You constantly think that you have not succeeded in your goals and that you are not worthy of anything good in life. Are you having trouble focusing on a single task without your mind drifting away? This can also be a warning sign of depression. When you cannot read the newspaper or watch something on TV, this means that your mind is tired and you have no power over it. You may also act as if you cannot perform as usual. You are talking and walking too slow and others start noticing that. However, sometimes depressed people experience just the opposite. They are overwhelmed and on edge all the time. Their agitation prevents them from concentrating on their tasks. Finally, depression often comes with dark thoughts of not wanting to live anymore. If you are experiencing such thoughts, then it is imperative to seek medical help. I cannot stress that enough.

ANGELA GRACE

After having clarified what depression feels like, now is the time to take it a step further and discuss how to crush it. I know it can be hard and often requires medication or therapy to move on in your life. Nevertheless, it is essential that you find the root of that problem that has tormented you all this time. Although it might sound controversial at first and it does not apply to all situations out there, I am sure this shift of your mindset is able to help you look at things from a different perspective. Sometimes all it takes is just to observe from a distance and notice the patterns that are formed in your life.

Ever since we were little children, we have been taught that having a problem was the best way to draw attention. When you were sick, your parents made you soup and cuddled you. They even let you watch TV more than you were allowed to on other days and of course, you skipped school. Does that ring any bell? Growing up, we continued acting like that. When we sought attention, what we did was act as if we were anxious, depressed, extremely sad and people came to the rescue. This has been a train of thought process that we kept adhering to, as it was effective. It brought the results we had anticipated.

I want you to take a moment and think about the deep roots of physical or mental ailments. They stem from deep inside our bodies and our minds. If not all of them, then their vast majority. When you are feeling down, hopeless, or unable to think of anything good, then you are in emotional turmoil. If you are capable of causing depression to yourself, you are able to generate a substantial amount of these intense emotions and thoughts in the wrong direction. These thoughts and emotions act against you and they poison you. Whatever the source of your physical or mental ailment, it essentially comes from within you. Imagine being so angry at someone for a few minutes. Hold on to that feeling of anger, resentment, and disgust. Do that in the form of a mental exercise every day. Over time, you will find it harder to return to your prior state. Instead, this negative feeling will slowly spread and try to take control. Don't let it. Set the necessary conditions for health and prosperity.

Try something else. If you are suffering from depression, there are situations that trigger all that negativity. Surrender completely to the present moment. Don't demand anything, as you are practicing dying. You die before you die if it makes sense. Does this situation now have the power to induce new negativity in your life and make you unhappy? Complete acceptance of this moment as this is. Even your thoughts are resistant to the situation. Allow the ego to surrender and die. Once the ego has dissolved, you will find acceptance. In several cases, surrendering is the only thing you need to let go of that horrible thought or memory that has caused all this mess in your mental health.

Depression is real and it can torment you unless you learn how to beat it. You cannot just sleep through it or ignore it until it goes away. This is a real issue that has been glooming people's lives for ages. It is in your power to fight back and not be the victim when it comes to your feelings. Do not get consumed by the negativity that is spreading like the plague inside you. Make the necessary changes in your life, so that depression has nowhere to hide. Do whatever it takes to lift your spirit and regain control over your life. Find your true meaning, your higher calling, the purpose that makes all other pieces of the puzzle suddenly click.

Below you will find some truly helpful tips that can make your life a lot more pleasurable. Remember that you are in control of the way you feel. When something doesn't suit you, change it until it does. When you are feeling down, go out there and find what makes your heart beat faster. Instead of falling into the trap of feeling miserable and blaming others for that misery, make it your goal to crush that misery and never experience it again. It is going to take time, it is going to be difficult, and still, it is worth pulling yourself out of this pit and into this wonderful world that is eagerly waiting for you to thrive!

Self-Care Tips

You should love yourself no matter what. Love and accept who you are unconditionally so that you unlock the beauty of your divine potential. This is your life and you should be living it exactly the way you want. This means that you focus on positive things, rather than hold grudges and seek revenge. If you do the latter, you will eventually be drowned in these negative emotions that make you feel terrible about yourself. It is a constant struggle to maintain that wide smile upon your face. However, this smile is worth every single battle.

Stop being resentful and jealous of other people's lives. First of all, you should be happy that others are blissful and filled with joy. You are on your path to get there and the universe has enough to provide for everyone in the world. It is not their fault that you are in different situations right now. Furthermore, when you do get to this magnificent moment of finding your higher calling in life and enjoying every moment to its fullest potential, you want others to be happy for you. Empathy is a virtue that enables you to see things more clearly. Do not poison your mind with envy, because it backfires and makes you feel miserable. Feel glad that others have conquered their goals and set your own goals even higher.

What you need to understand is that you cannot be perfect in every little thing you do. Blaming yourself for not being good enough does not get you anywhere. Instead, it prevents you from accomplishing all those amazing things you are destined to accomplish in your life. Do not underestimate your value. Every individual has been given a special gift and it is up to you to discover yours,

SPIRITUAL GROWTH FOR WOMEN

exploring your talents, and ultimately finding out what your true calling is. Do not be defensive against others, in an attempt to justify your performance.

It is all a matter of habit. In your daily routine, here are some things that can help you out crush depression and welcome joy into your life. Be sure to implement them into your daily routine, so that you enjoy a fulfilled existence that oozes with bliss and joy, hope, and above anything else, love:

- Set realistic goals: You cannot expect to lose 30 pounds, learn how to speak Italian, or master the art of cooking overnight. Give yourself time and ease into it. Set attainable goals that you can adhere to. Divide your long-term goals into smaller chunks, celebrating milestones and evaluating your progress as you go. This will help you remain motivated and avoid getting discouraged by slow results.
- Reward yourself: When you do something nice, give yourself a reward. Go out and buy that dress after losing 10 pounds. Go get a new haircut, sip on a relaxing chamomile tea or find the time to read a favorite book. Dedicate some time to yourself, so that you feel amazing and accomplished. It doesn't even have to be something fancy. Just a pat on your shoulder and a kind word will be appreciated.
- Indulge in pleasurable activities: What makes your heart spark and what keeps you motivated? Listen to music, take long bubble baths, cook with your loved ones, go out for a leisurely walk in nature. Being outdoors definitely helps lift your spirit. Let the sunshine gently caress your skin or feel the raindrops falling on your face. Nature is wonderful if you take the time and watch closely the wonders that happen all the time.

59

- Practice gratitude: There are so many things you should be grateful for in your life. Do you ever give thanks for all that has come your way so far? You woke up this morning breathing and this is a blessing on its own. Take a moment and think of what you are grateful for. This is a great wake-up call for all those people who are on the verge of giving up. Don't take anything for granted and enjoy every single day you get to be awesome.
- Meditate: Meditation can be proven extremely helpful if you want to relax and let go of the tension or troubles that have clouded your judgment. In this way, you will perfect your skills of being in the present moment and appreciating every second. Nothing is as important as here and now. Don't fret over things you cannot control. Be present at the moment and let your mind drift away, wandering off to your spiritual explorations.
- Get enough sleep: When your body and mind do not get enough rest, imbalances are bound to happen. Make sure that you implement a sleep routine that enables you to rest for at least 7 to 8 hours per day. Abstain from blue light, make yourself a soothing herbal tea, take a relaxing shower, visualize what you want to manifest in life, and goodnight!
- Change your diet: We are what we eat. Therefore, you need to reassess your dietary patterns and make necessary modifications to boost your health and wellness. Choose fish, nuts, and probiotics, along with fresh leafy vegetables and seasonal fruit. Avoid sugar and refined carbohydrates, as well as overly processed foods. Cut down on your alcohol and coffee intake for optimal benefits. Over time, your body will be grateful for your choices.
- Be more social: Be around people who lift your spirit, rather than surround yourself with people who bring you

SPIRITUAL GROWTH FOR WOMEN

down. You should opt for those people with an elevated vibrational frequency, as they will make it easier for you to attract the same emotions in your life. Be open and talk to others honestly without any hidden agenda. Finally, get out of your comfort zone and talk to people you don't even know. It can be fun!

- Exercise more: By working out more frequently, you release the tension from your body and you enjoy the production of endorphins. These are hormones that make you feel happier. Moreover, exercise allows you to be more sociable, enhances your self-esteem, and optimizes your health. Need I say anything else?
- Laugh more: Laughter relaxes your entire body, triggers the release of endorphins, and enhances your immune system. It lightens your mood, allowing you to get rid of the tension and it makes you feel good right away. Laugh out loud, smile whenever possible, and don't let that frown get you down.

8

EMPOWER YOURSELF, EMPOWER YOUR FAMILY

Do you often feel the need to shy away from a challenge? Do you second-doubt yourself, even when making decisions you are certain of? You are not alone in this. Many women have been used to less important roles in their life. They have become accustomed to that feeling of insecurity shadowing their every move. As a result, it is hard for them to believe in their infinite power. It is difficult to change their mindset in a way that promotes spiritual growth and exponential empowerment.

One of the fundamental issues you will be confronted with within your life is control. When you find yourself in an unknown environment, instinctively you become more agitated. Your senses are on alert so that you identify these unfamiliar details that help you interpret your surroundings. This is a great tool for your survival, but it can hinder your path towards self-actualization. Unless you let go of your strive to control everything in life, you can never feel safe within your limitations.

Remember that you are the co-creator of everything that happens in your life and you are able to formulate changes for and around you. This doesn't mean that you hold full accountability for whatever happens in your life and in the life of those around you.

SPIRITUAL GROWTH FOR WOMEN

Nobody has that power. However, you are equipped with tools that contribute to your journey. If you use those tools properly, you will get the opportunity to forge your life in a way that pleases you. In a different situation, you are found weak and helpless.

Some women lose faith in themselves when compared with men. In the back of their mind, they believe they cannot compete with them. Still, it is important to be aligned with your nature. There are feminine traits within you that define your personality, such as intuition and empathy, compassion, and love. At the same time, as a woman, you also possess the masculine traits of logic and practicality. By acknowledging your dual self and embracing both your feminine and masculine side, you can change your life far beyond gender biases.

You teach others how to treat you, based on what you accept, what you stop, and what you reinforce. No one has complete control. When people try to please others all the time, this might come as a response to their not knowing who they truly are. Before moving forward with your life, you need to determine who you want to be. What do you want to become? Are you an artist, a scientist, a philosopher, a teacher, or a builder? What do you wish to create? What is your true purpose in life? Unless you clearly define these aspects of your being, you cannot experience wholeness. You will spend your days in anticipation of a brighter future that may not arrive for you, since you do not actually know what to attract in your life.

Life can be hard on so many different levels. Finding yourself in a complicated life seems unattainable, but it is crucial for your well-being. There must be characteristics of yours that do not appeal to you, things you would like to change but cannot find the courage to do so. It would be great to be bold and daring, but this is not the way the world operates. Instead, you must take it one step at a time. Take that first step towards changing your life and commit to your endeavor. Try hard until you succeed in accomplishing that very goal you have set.

63

ANGELA GRACE

Upon completing this first task, you will realize how many possibilities unfold before your eyes. Life is filled with surprises and endless opportunities for you to grow spiritually. More often than not, this revelation only comes after hard work and dedication to your goals. You need to labor before seeing that marvelous transformation in your life. But when it does, everything suddenly clicks and you discover your true purpose. Part of that discovery is the acknowledgment that you should put yourself first, no matter if it fits your former philosophy.

PUTTING YOURSELF FIRST

You are the representation of God in your life. It is not selfish to put yourself first, as you need to be of service to others. How can you be of service to them if you do not thrive personally? Unless you take care of yourself and your needs, you will eventually burn out and feel drained of your energy. This can happen from one moment to the next and the repercussions will be awful. Even if you have the will to serve humanity, your body and spirit will not help you. Instead, you will be limited as to what you can achieve. This doesn't benefit anyone in the long run.

When you take care of yourself and remain healthy, whole, and fulfilled, you can go ahead and focus on how to make the world a better place. This is in no way an indication of disregarding people around you. On the contrary, it is your will to serve others that drives you to make the best of yourself. You want your life to be whole and complete so that you can devote your entire self towards doing good for others. Unless you have satisfied your needs and provided for yourself, you cannot commit to helping the people around you.

Most women have taken on too many roles within their life. They are mothers and spouses, friends and lovers, business associates, helpers, nurses, and caretakers. It is a hectic ride just to make sure that they make it through the day in one piece. Modern

SPIRITUAL GROWTH FOR WOMEN

society dictates that women are super tools, able to deliver every-thing they are asked to with no complaints and no glitches. However, this always takes a toll on them. High expectations can be flattering at first, but in the end, they reveal the ugly truth. They reveal that certain beliefs are simply out of this world, unable to be met no matter how hard one may try.

There is a wide misconception as to the extent of giving uncon-ditionally. You should make that clear in your mind that there should be a thin line you never cross when giving. Many people claim that you should sacrifice your own content, in order to give to the community. If you do that and deprive yourself of something vital, then the person receiving your help is turned into a thief. In fact, they might not even know that they are stealing something so crucial for your existence. They don't deserve to be put in that posi-tion, do they?

The majority of your focus is on other people. Your needs are pushed down and they are always second. On the surface, every-thing may look the same. Nothing is wrong. However, by denying yourself on the long haul to serve others, you sabotage yourself. Over time, you might feel afflicted by your compelling need to put other people first. Ignoring your personal interests, your desires, and true longings, you consider yourself inferior to others. Is this what you want to project to the world? When you deny your own needs, you are not in the position to help others, and sooner or later you are going to discover that through your own behavior.

I know putting yourself first may contradict everything you have been raised to do in your life. All these years, you have been taught to give and provide for the community. Your needs are not as important as the bigger picture. Yet, recall the last time you were on an airplane. Just before taking off, what did the flight attendants instruct you to do? They explained that in case of an emergency, you should first provide yourself with an oxygen mask and a vest. Then, after having made sure that you are safe, you can tend to those next to you. Otherwise, you cannot be of any

ANGELA GRACE

real service to them, as you will most likely have lost consciousness.

Therefore, it is of the essence to give yourself everything for a happy and healthy life. Be whole and content, fulfilled and energized, so that you can serve others in the best possible manner. Everybody wins that way. By putting yourself first, you become empowered and you are able to help others in a much more meaningful way. If you were left to feel miserable, you would not have the same strength or willingness to strive for greatness. Everyday problems would get in the way and distract you from your higher purpose in life.

You can use the power of affirmations to reinforce your conviction of putting yourself before others in life. Repeat the following affirmations, so as to enhance your beliefs that your life matters and you should love, accept and honor yourself completely:

- Putting myself first is the best way to serve others.
- I love and nurture myself because I deserve to be.
- I am worthy of serving my own needs.
- I am worthy of self-love.
- When I serve my needs, I am more energized to help others with their needs.
- Loving and taking care of myself is the best thing to do for myself and everyone else.
- I will not feel guilty for putting myself first.
- I have the power to change my world and the world of others.
- I believe in myself and I value myself more than anything in the world.
- I deserve all that is good.
- I am receiving everything that is good so that I can give back goodness to the world.

Take a look at these phrases. They all reflect how you should feel about yourself. Don't feel guilty because of your need to prioritize your well-being. This is the prerequisite for delivering amazing services to those around you. Love yourself and tend to your needs first, so that you are able to help all others in your surroundings in the best way possible. Of course, it all starts with the family.

Empowering Your Family

By pursuing your personal needs and desires, you are actually setting an example in your family. You are leading by example, inspiring them to do the same thing. Happiness should not be considered a sin or something you should shy away from. On the contrary, taking care of yourself needs to be of the highest priority in your life. Your family will notice how amazing your life is after nurturing your body, your soul, and your mind. They will acknowledge how virtuous your path has been and they will want to walk right by your side. They will be encouraged to pursue their true passions and loves in their own life.

When you settle for a life that does not reward you, others notice that. Unless you show the world around you how much you value yourself, others will take you for granted and never appreciate what you deserve. This is not good for the family dynamics. You need to be a source of inspiration to your significant other, your children, and your loved ones. You can only do that if you respect yourself and accept who you really are. If you keep pushing yourself down, you are not doing anyone a favor. Make yourself a priority, so as to get the energy and will be required to help your family thrive.

Teach them what it feels like to be unstoppable. Teach them love and compassion, solidarity and respect, self-confidence, and the belief in a higher power. Show them the way to pursue their goals in a healthy, non-competitive way that promotes bliss and joy for everyone. As your family sees your impressive life transformation, they will follow in your footsteps and yearn for such changes to happen to them, too. They will listen to you, as you are walking them on a journey towards self-awareness and spiritual growth.

If you diminish yourself in front of your family, they will do the same and they will learn that it is OK to sacrifice for others. They will never get appreciated for what they offer and they will never feel good enough. Why would you condemn your family in an endless vortex of negative feelings including self-guilt, shame, and inferiority complexes? On the contrary, you should give them the opportunity to benefit from healthy role models that they can then adjust to their own reality.

Use your family, loved ones, and friends as motivation for you to heal yourself. Be the change you want to be in the world and instill that in your family. Encourage them to stand up for what they believe, teaching them that it is great to express themselves and demand what is rightfully theirs. At the same time, teach them to be compassionate and empathize with other people. Allow them to experiment until they find their higher purpose in life. Once they do, motivate them to master their skills and go after their dreams. Show them how to live their lives blissfully, wholeheartedly, and meaningfully.

Be there for your family, as they will be there for you. Make sure that your needs and feelings are expressed just as much as the other members of the family. Be full in your life, so that the rest of your family can see what it feels like. If you are feeling the urge to dictate to others what they should do, resist that urge with your entire strength. There is a huge difference between telling someone how to do things and educating them about the choices that they are going to make. In the former case, you risk watching your behavior backfire at you. They might do the exact opposite thing, just out of spite or resentment. In the latter, though, you give them tools they can use for life.

Make sure that your family knows how much you support them. Tell each member of your family how important they are to the family unit and let them know you love them unconditionally. You never want anyone to feel left out. This can be catastrophic as to the family dynamics since it is bound to raise conflicts and negative emotions. You need to maintain harmony within the family. Be

SPIRITUAL GROWTH FOR WOMEN

open and honest about all aspects of the family, whether they include sensitive matters or not. Only through honesty and transparency can you build on solid ground and lay strong foundations.

Last but not least, remember that no one is the victim. Do not consider yourself the victim, even if you have been accustomed to such a role within the family. Choose the path of justice, when everything is discussed together as a whole. You will have disagreements and fights at some point along the road, but you must never reach extremes. Everybody is equal within the family. Instill that in your family and join them in shared experiences that benefit all of you for life.

9

PERSEVERANCE, DISCIPLINE, AND EMPOWERMENT FOR THE SPIRITUALLY POWERFUL WOMAN (DON'T QUIT!)

I am well aware that everybody in this world has dreams. Yet, how many of these people are willing to do what it takes for those dreams to become real? In order to bring any dream to fruition, you must have self-discipline. Some people may resent the term, but it is a wonderful concept. You forego the temporary pleasure and you exchange it for long-term respect. Personally, I think this is a great deal. Instead of being happy for an hour and then frowning and feeling miserable all day, you aim higher and it pays off in the long run.

We go about in our lives thinking that the world is against us when actually we continuously choose to self-sabotage. What we eat and what we drink, how we spend our days, all these elements shape our everyday life and determine whether we are destined for greatness or settling for mediocrity. See what happens when you take full ownership of everything. You will be in control of your life and you will have no one to blame. This is a liberating feeling, setting your priorities straight and ultimately awakening you from your sleep. Why would you ever place control of your life over other people's hands? Why would you do that to yourself?

I know there are times when life becomes overwhelming. There

SPIRITUAL GROWTH FOR WOMEN

are so many things that can go wrong. All these things seem out of your hand. How can you interfere with the future and what it holds for you? You are an observer to your life, waiting for bad things to happen and trying to hold someone else responsible. However, you are still in control of your reactions. Even if the worst stuff has happened in your life, you are not alone. All these wonderful people around you have their own baggage to deal with. Some have given up and have lost all hope. Yet, there are people who still believe in a better future. Guess who live their life to its fullest potential.

Overcoming hardships can be tough, I get it. Problems take over and they hardly give you a moment to rest your mind. They demand your uninterrupted attention and you feel trapped. Take a step back and observe your life from a distance. What do you see? You are alive, you are healthy, you are surrounded by loved ones, you have a job that pays the bills and brings food on the table, you have a roof over your head, a car, or a house by the sea. Of course, these are generic observations and do not apply to us all. Nevertheless, by taking a step back and observing from a distance, it is certain that you are going to count more blessings than what you originally thought you had in your life.

With all these blessings in your life, why would you ever get discouraged? There are a lot of things worth fighting for. Fight for those things. If you feel deprived of something specific, do your best and do not stop until you get it. Commit to this goal and excel at how to achieve this goal. If it is something too complex or time-consuming, then break it down into smaller parts and focus on how to accomplish each and every single one of them. Nothing is impossible unless your mind has decided that it is.

Do not reject self-discipline for fear it brings out the worst in you. In fact, this could not be further from the truth. When you discipline yourself, you actually bring out the best in you. You learn that you have complete power over the things you do, your thoughts, and reactions. This is a true revelation. By mastering the art of discipline, you can make the right decisions and be proud of them. You will honor those decisions, as they will be in your best interest. Instead of leaving things to chance or instinct, you will now have a solid compass to guide you.

Imagine that you have now returned home after a long day at the office. You are famished because you didn't get the chance to eat. When you open the fridge, you see a pizza with your name on it. I am sure your first reaction is to take the pizza box out and eat the whole thing. It is just the way you like it and you haven't eaten anything all day. However, when you learn how to discipline yourself, you will think that you love yourself too much to sabotage them like that. After eating the pizza, you will be bloated and you will feel awful. You will also feel guilty about overeating and you will loathe yourself for giving in to temptation once more.

As you can see, by being disciplined you essentially push yourself to reach that higher self. It is the ultimate act of kindness and thus should be treated as such. On the contrary, you need to work on dealing with negative aspects of your life that hinder your progress. Procrastination is a key element that can stall your spiritual growth due to its great impact on your everyday life. By definition, procrastination is what prevents you from engaging in important things and instead pushes you to waste time on trivial activities. You tend to overlook deadlines and underestimate the severity of your actions until it is too late.

Even when you do realize that procrastination must be rejected, it is too hard to get over it. Something inside you makes you give in to the temporary bliss of procrastinating, getting pleasure out of meaningful activities that offer you nothing in the long term. You end up feeling guilty and ashamed that you had not adhered to the timeline, exactly like you should have done if you wanted to finish a project on time. What is interesting about procrastination is that it holds great power over you and therefore you feel as if you were compelled to obey, when that little voice inside your mind suggests procrastinating. It is happening right there and you are drawn into a behavioral pattern that you acknowledge is bad for you. Still, you do it and you postpone your worries for when reality sets in (Saiisha, 2020).

ON THE PATH OF SPIRITUAL GROWTH

Life is hard and the road ahead is filled with obstacles that challenge you along the way. When faced with all these difficulties, you might feel like giving up. Even though you tried, nothing seems to change. It is futile to go into all this trouble and get nothing in return. There is no improvement whatsoever, no matter how hard you work towards growing spiritually and improving your life. Everything you have visualized seems to be fading away, leaving nothing else other than disappointment and despair.

This is a turning point for you. Despite what your impulse might be, you need to be strong. Don't quit, even when you go against all odds. Never abandon your spiritual practice and growth. It is at that moment when you are gasping for air that the true wonders appear. When you persevere, sooner or later you get the rewards you have been craving for. You need to have faith in the higher power so that you withstand the hardships and remain true to your goals. Life is meant to be hard. It is meant to be painful. At times, life is unfair and it torments you in ways you cannot handle.

However, you pull through and watch yourself as you are transformed into this wonderful being. You are an infinite being with immense power and endless possibilities revealed before you when you least expect them. Why would you want to give up after all the pain you have been through? No one has claimed that the journey is easy. It is not all roses and flowers. Instead, there is pain and suffering. You know it all too well. Still, what lies on the other side of the road is what you have been preparing yourself to experience. What is waiting for you on the other side is a true masterpiece. It is a miracle no words can describe it in its entirety.

The road to your spiritual growth comes with a lot of challenges. You need to devote your time and energy wholeheartedly, in order to push forward and progress. It is essential that you study and experiment until you find what works for you. Above all, you must believe and have faith that there is a higher power shining bright and guiding you in this journey. Even if at first what you try seems uncomfortable, give it a chance. You will be expected to step out of your comfort zone and see things from a new perspective. Be open-minded and committed to your goals.

Feel free to investigate, do your research and draw your conclusions. Delve in the philosophies of the Orient, read a lot, and surround yourself with like-minded people. They will lift your spirit and show you the way to expand, rather than retract in life. They will support and inspire you, leading you to the discovery of your inner self. Do not lose hope when things do not work out as planned. Remember that the universe always knows best. Be focused on your end destination and enjoy the ride until you get there.

Exercises to Grow Spiritually

Deep breathing is essential for your spiritual self. You need to discover the hidden power within your breathing. Yoga is great in unveiling the potential of your lungs and respiratory system, bringing you to a state of deep relaxation. Pranayama yoga allows you to promote spiritual growth through simple yet greatly effective exercises. Below I will describe four deep breathing exercises that I have found extremely helpful.

Starting with the basics, you need to practice the fundamental

SPIRITUAL GROWTH FOR WOMEN

yogi deep breathing exercise in pranayama yoga. In order to master it fully, you must sit down comfortably and cross your legs. Your spine needs to be upright so that your chakras create a straight virtual pillar from the ground. Keep your feet connected to each other and close your eyes. Concentrate on your breathing. When you inhale through the nose, you should feel the air slowly filling your belly and then moving upwards to your lungs. This will allow you to breathe fresh air into your root, sacral, and solar plexus chakras. Hold your breath for a few seconds and then exhale through the mouth until your body empties completely.

You need to sit down, cross-legged, and with your palms on your lap facing upwards. This is the ultimate receiving pose. Take your right hand and bend the index and middle finger. With the thumb and the little finger, you will block your nostrils when it is needed. Press your right nostril with your thumb and inhale non-stop until you count to four. Then retain the air inside your lungs until you count to sixteen. You will have to block your left nostril with your little finger too, preventing the air from escaping your nose. When you are done, free your right nostril and exhale until you count to eight. Repeat on the other side, by pressing your left nostril and following the same steps.

For the next deep breathing exercise, imagine you have a mirror right in front of your face. You want to fog that mirror through your breath. I am sure you are familiar with this cute experiment. In this case, there is no mirror and you keep your mouth closed. Breathe in deeply and then exhale without opening your mouth, causing a small constriction in your throat. You might feel strange with the sound your throat produces at first, but you get used to it over time. It sounds like subtle snoring or like the gentle waves of the ocean on the shore. The more you practice, the longer you are going to last during the exhalation step.

The fourth and last exercise is equally relaxing. You sit cross-legged again and you place your index fingers on the cartilage of your ears. You press the cartilage and you inhale through the nose.

75

ANGELA GRACE

As you exhale through the mouth, you produce sounds just like a hummingbird. These sounds come straight from your nose and they allow your body to become aligned with the energy of the universe. You feel the vibration from within you, as you are producing these sounds. Again, through practice, you learn how to make your exhaling last longer for optimal results.

Besides yoga, you can also use a power affirmation journal. This is a great way to inspire positive self-reflection, by writing down motivational affirmations in your journal to promote empowerment and spiritual growth. You are free to get a notebook that you love turning to on a daily basis, dedicating a few minutes to focus on those aspects of your life you wish to boost. It can be your career or your personal relationships, your school performance, or fears that you have not yet dealt with. Just write down everything that is on your mind and be positive. Ooze with optimism as you are writing down so that you can return to your scripts and read them to feel empowered.

Always include positive affirmations about yourself while journaling. You should write down your best features and traits that you love about yourself, as well as enhance your confidence through projecting things you wish you possessed. For instance, you can write that you are worthy of accomplishing anything you set your mind on. This is something that you firmly believe. You can also write that you are a great motivational speaker, even though getting up and talking in front of people makes you shiver with fear. If this is something that you want to achieve, then write about it and project it to the world.

Apart from yoga and journaling, a great way to boost your spiritual growth is to mindfully meditate. You can use your mind to wander off to places where you have never been, discovering your inner balance and finding your spiritual self. It is amazing what the mind can accomplish if you just let it. You need to find a quiet and comfortable place so that you can relax completely and let go of any worries or tension. Without any distractions, you can tap into

76

SPIRITUAL GROWTH FOR WOMEN

your spiritual self and drift away in pursuit of your infinite potential.

Close your eyes or just focus your gaze on a single thing, just breathing deeply and being in the present moment. This will allow you to transcend into a different dimension and follow your spirit where it takes you. To get optimal results, you can light scented candles or incense prior to the meditation. Certain types of soothing music also help you get in that relaxed state of mind that promotes self-growth. As you are breathing deeply, you find yourself in a dream place. A place that only exists in your dreams and it is the perfect place for you to stay in. This place is magnificent and you feel blessed for being there.

Take in every single detail about this place. When you finish observing it, shift your focus on a great white light shining upon you. It is shining right down on you from the sky. This light is astonishing. Pure white bliss showers you and makes you feel ecstatic. It is this bright light that fills you with energy and allows you to see clearly. You are joyful at this moment. You feel your energy centers light up vividly, as they are radiating with that abundant light. Each energy center opens up and spins like a wheel so brightly, maintaining its own distinct color. They are all astonishingly beautiful, creating a rainbow with all their chromatic hues blended together.

As that light continues to shine through you, you notice your own aura expanding. It is a lovely aura, healthy-looking and bright. It has become thick and dense, colorful and filled with life. This aura protects you and allows you to vibrate at an elevated frequency, attracting all the marvelous things that you want to manifest in your life. That aura has been cleansed by the abundant light coming from the sky and you feel its beneficial power embracing you. Stay in this moment for as long as you like, enjoying the peace and calmness, the refreshing cleanse of your energy centers, and the infinite power flowing through you.

When you want to return to your current reality, just open your

ANGELA GRACE

eyes and slowly move your legs and hands. You will notice a slight tingling sensation all over your body. Through this mindful meditation, you will become much more receptive to the spiritual aspects of your existence. You will be able to communicate with the universe, deeply connected to the world. More than that, you will have the opportunity to pursue your higher self through a wonderful journey that takes you to your ultimate sanctuary. It is a splendid meditation that you are welcome to use anytime you need to lift your spirit, let go of stagnant energy and restore your inner balance.

❧ 10 ❧
AMAZING GUIDED MEDITATIONS TO SUPERCHARGE YOUR SPIRITUAL GROWTH

Meditation can be a powerful tool in your hands. If you use it wisely, you will be able to unfold the mysteries of the universe and reach the depths of your existence. Below I have created five special guided meditations for you. They have been categorized according to what they target. These meditations will help you overcome any boundaries of your physical body and your mind, enabling you to tap into your divine feminine energy. From that point, you will have the opportunity to explore your spirituality and gain knowledge of magnificent things along the way.

Before starting any of those meditating sessions, you need to choose the perfect setting. It can be your bedroom, the living room, or even the balcony. You can also meditate outdoors, as being closer to nature certainly adds to your experience. However, it is best to control your environment and keep it clean. Clutter and dirt can create energy blocks that prevent you from enjoying the benefits of meditation to the fullest. Wear comfortable clothes and create a soothing atmosphere. You can use scented candles or incense and soft music that promotes relaxation.

Make sure that you find a time within the day when you don't get interrupted. It is of paramount importance to maintain your

ANGELA GRACE

calmness throughout the meditation, undisturbed by anyone or anything. Some people choose to meditate early in the morning before they start their day, whereas others prefer nighttime. The choice is entirely yours. Practice mindful meditation and you will see that every single time you become even more concentrated.

GUIDED MEDITATION TO ACCOMPLISH WHOLENESS

Feeling whole is of the essence in your journey towards spiritual growth. This meditation will allow you to accomplish wholeness and connect to the universe. Sit somewhere comfortable and allow yourself to relax. Make sure that you have plenty of time to dedicate to yourself and close your eyes.

Breathe deeply, inhaling through the nose and exhaling through the mouth. Every breath you take paves the way towards wholeness. It is part of your journey and you need to embrace it. Become part of the cosmos and fill with that magnificent energy. With every breath, you become more in tune with that energy around you. Feel the truth of your spiritual identity, feel the truth of your wholeness. Choose to see the larger picture.

Imagine a tree. Focus on its entirety and try to notice every single detail. Notice the roots as they emerge from deep underneath the surface. Watch the tree trunk with the numerous lines that reveal its age, its past, its experiences. Observe the tree leaves as they are dancing to the beat of the winds. Some of the leaves fall down to the ground, still dancing to that beat. Observe it closely and continue breathing in deeply, feeling your whole body filled with that refreshing air.

Always keep in mind that the choices of today pave your tomorrow. Today choose to celebrate your special identity within your spiritual wholeness. Feel that breath of life coming from the eternal tree to your body. Appreciate this aspect of your existence. Take deep breaths and notice how the air brings life into every single cell within your body, from head to toe. It is a great feeling, connecting

SPIRITUAL GROWTH FOR WOMEN

you with nature and its wonders. Feel the softness, the relaxation, the absolute peace all around you. Everything is whole. You are whole.

Inhale the energy and experience self-assurance that everything is going to be alright. Exhale and celebrate wholeness, peace, and serenity. Believe in yourself. You are worthy to be happy and whole in your life. Expand your chest as you are breathing deeply and let go of any negative thoughts from within you. The spirits are here to guide you in your journey. They fill you with the energy you need to achieve your greatness. They are graceful and shower you with grace, too. Your tomorrow will be fulfilling and blessed.

Think of all the hard work you have been doing. Reward yourself for all that hard work. You know that it spreads throughout humanity, touching others in the most wonderful way. Remember your own truth and your own identity. You are a blessed part of the universe. Celebrate your individual wholeness within the oneness of the cosmos. Inhale all the goodness in life and exhale compassion, peace, and harmony. Inhale self-assurance and exhale your truth.

Bring awareness to your body and the quality of your mind. Notice if your body is holding on to tension or if it is fully relaxed. Recognize your full body, your spirit, and your mind as a whole. Every part of your existence is showered with light. Nothing will ever be in the darkness. You are full of light and you radiate that light to the world around you. In fact, you are a beacon of light that brings hope and compassion to those who need it. Glow in that abundant light that is shining from the highest divine spirits to you. Appreciate that light, accept it gratefully.

Acknowledge that everything you are doing is perfect and you are exactly where you wanted to be. With every inhale, repeat to yourself that you are worthy. As you are exhaling, repeat to yourself that you are enough. Illustrate the perfection of your existence. "I am worthy" with every inhale and "I am enough" with every exhale. Let go of everything that no longer serves. Notice your thoughts as they drift away from your mind and let them go. Let them float

81

effortlessly up in the sky. You are whole, you are deeply connected to the universe.

Take a nice deep breath of gratitude, exhaling it so that it permeates everything around you. Allow your body to feel all that magnificent energy from the abundant divine light and then breathe it back to the world. Slowly open your eyes and regain consciousness. You will feel lighter and happier, more profoundly connected to that mystical eternal power that holds everything together.

GUIDED MEDITATION FOR CLEANSING CHAKRAS

When you want to unblock your energy centers from stagnant energy that has accumulated and is now hindering your spiritual growth, you can use this guided meditation. Choose a peaceful setting, sit comfortably with your back straight, and dim the lights.

Bring awareness to your body and become fully centered. Calm down and realize that this time is dedicated to your healing. Allow yourself to relax, while maintaining the upright position of your back. Find the inner peacefulness that you carry within you. You are becoming calm, peaceful, and relaxed. Become aware that you are a light body in human form. Start to sense a white glowing light all around you. Even if you have never looked, this light is always there. Become aware of this radiant light surrounding you.

This light is emanating from your own body, as you are its creator. You are radiant and you are shining brightly from head to toe. Feel how energizing it is to glow and allow yourself to acknowledge your powerful white light energy. Be mindful of its powerful potential. Your white light is divided into your seven chakras in the colors of the rainbow. These energy centers are located within your body along your spine, connecting you to the cosmos. Bring your awareness to your root chakra. It radiates with red light from the base of your spine. Take some deep slow breaths to cleanse your root chakra, inhaling through the nose and exhaling through the mouth.

SPIRITUAL GROWTH FOR WOMEN

Move up to the area right below your navel to your sacral chakra that glows in orange color light. Focus your attention there. Breathe in and out white light energy through your sacral chakra. Repeat that as many times as you like until you see that orange chakra beaming with orange light. You step into self-awareness and move upwards to your solar plexus chakra. This energy center shines in yellow. Again, breathe in and out white light energy to cleanse this chakra. When it glows brightly, your solar plexus chakra has been cleansed.

When you are ready, move a little up to the heart chakra at the center of your chest, slightly above your heart. This energy center shines in a magnificent green light. Draw your attention to it and cleanse it through your abundant white light energy. Take deep breaths, breathing in through the nose and out through the mouth. Purify any stagnant energy until you see the heart chakra glowing astonishingly. Become aware now of your throat chakra, the blue energy center located at your throat. Begin your breathing, exactly like you did with the other chakras before that. Allow the white light to shine through and cleanse the throat chakra until you notice that radiant blue light.

It is time to bring your attention to the third eye chakra at the center of your heart right between your eyebrows. Begin breathing in and out your healing white light, taking as much time as needed for you to purify it completely. Feel the white light bathing the third eye chakra until it has washed away all the energy blocks that have diminished its power. When you notice the indigo color of that energy center shine brightly, you have unblocked it perfectly. Finally, move your focus on your crown chakra. This is the energy center that is placed just above the top of your head. Take a few deep breaths now, as this chakra is cleansed and starts shining in vivid violet light all around you. By completing all these seven rounds of chakra cleansing, you can sigh with relief and enjoy the marvelous results starting from within.

Return to your initial visualization of abundant white light energy surrounding your body now. See and sense that the totality of you is shining brighter than ever before. You are so luminous, vivid, and radiant. Stay in this state for a few moments and be present, enjoying this wonderful experience. Feel the energy and the inspiration, as you are showered with cosmic love. The white light shines brightly all around your body, expanding to the universe. Your seven chakras have been cleansed and they are now beacons of light, flowing through you and outward to the universe. Open your eyes when you feel ready.

GUIDED MEDITATION FOR MASTERING PERSEVERANCE

Through this mindful meditation, you will find a way to keep yourself motivated and never give up. By mastering perseverance, you will be able to follow your dreams and ultimately achieve them, no matter how hard they might seem at first. This is a powerful meditation, meant to ignite the spark within you.

Close your eyes and let your mind wander for a while. After a few moments, bring awareness to your breath. Breathe in through the nose for a count of five and then breathe out through the mouth as you count until five. Repeat that a few times until you become fully relaxed. Feel your muscles let go of any tension that has been piling up. Notice every part of your body. Make sure that you are balanced and your body is ready to surrender to absolute serenity.

Allow yourself to release all expectations that you have created through change. Change is never easy, but you can do anything. Breathe in and out as you are focusing on the fact that you can do this. It doesn't matter how complex the endeavor, it doesn't matter how many obstacles come up along the way, and in the end, you are going to succeed in this. You are meant to succeed and bring your dreams to fruition.

What emotions are you feeling right now? Release all the negative emotions that you may be experiencing and welcome the posi-

SPIRITUAL GROWTH FOR WOMEN

tive feelings that have come your way. Acknowledge that you are an infinite being and that anything is possible. Focus on the connection between your mind and your body. As you are doing that, repeat the following affirmation: *"I see the invisible, I feel the intangible, and I can achieve the impossible."*

Continue breathing in and out. Remember that you are a woman. You are an exceptional being that is capable of glorious things. You have the power to create life and you can overcome any obstacle. It is in your hands to achieve anything you set your mind on. You can persevere and stick to your goals. Know that you can trust yourself. You are worthy of accomplishing your goals, no matter how unattainable they might seem. There is nothing in this world that should hold you back or make you retreat.

Even though there may be times when you feel afraid, repeat the following: *"I can overcome any barriers. I am able to achieve anything in life. There is nothing that can stop me from my journey towards self-growth. I am unstoppable."* Observe any negative thought or emotion that emerges as you are repeating those words. Breathe deeply and slowly as you are putting an end to self-doubt. You are a powerful woman and you ought to pursue your true calling in life. Don't let anything get in the way.

Try to visualize your dreams. What emotions are they bringing to the surface? Are you willing to conquer your dreams or have you been convinced that you cannot make them happen? Any dream of yours can become reality. You can manifest it into the world and enjoy this feeling of accomplishment. No mountain is high enough for you to climb on, because you deserve to reach any goal of yours that you have projected into this world. Believe in your immense power. You are a creature of this universe and you hold infinite power within you.

Feel those negative thoughts and feelings slip away and leave your body. Watch them as they leave your mind and allow you to breathe. Feel the energy of positive emotions and thoughts setting in, making you understand your potential. You will not give up,

ANGELA GRACE

because the universe is going to guide you through the process of pursuing your dreams. The spirits will be right by your side along the way. Feel them as they are shining down on you, protecting you from all harm.

When you are ready, resume awareness of your physical body. Open your eyes gently and allow your body to awaken refreshed and relaxed. Know that you can always return to this guided meditation when you lack the motivation to persevere. When you feel intimidated by the magnitude of an endeavor, you can always return to your roots and seek guidance within your infinite divine self.

GUIDED MEDITATION FOR SPIRITUAL GROWTH

If you are determined to delve into the mysteries of spirituality, then this guided meditation is a great tool that enables you to reach that profound life, shifting your mind and body forward. Sit down in a comfortable position with your palms on your lap facing upwards. In this way, you will be able to receive all those amazing things from the universe.

Close your eyes and breathe deeply. Follow the air filling your throat, your chest, and the abdominal area. Then follow it as it is slowly released back into the world. This meditation is your connection to the higher power, God, or the universe. This connection is your guide. Become aware of this guide and picture them in living form. How do they look? Observe every single detail, every single feature within their body and face. Your guide resides within you and you now have the opportunity to see exactly what they look like. How magnificent is that creature? Indeed, this is your higher self and therefore knows everything. They have the answer to all questions, both those who have been asked and those who have been left unspoken.

This creature makes you feel safe about your decisions. You gain confidence by knowing that you have your guide right next to you, leading you towards enlightenment. It is certain that your choices

86

SPIRITUAL GROWTH FOR WOMEN

will be the best that you can make, given that your guide will have inspired you. You are driven by something that feels overpowering, yet that force is within you. You have created it and you are receiving it. Even if you were afraid to decide about a significant event in your life, now it all looks clearer. You have the power to decide prudently, based on absolute knowledge. There is nothing in this world that can make you feel uncertain, dubious, doubtful of the validity of your judgment.

Be aware of connecting to that creature, while being grounded and fully centered. Now picture yourself standing side by side in a special place. This is your dreamland, the ultimate space where you would like to be. It can be anywhere in the world or it might exist only in your fantasy. It is your sanctuary and it is perfectly peaceful. You are just sitting there being present. You are sitting side by side with your guide and you are enjoying the moment. Suddenly, you realize that you have the ability to tap into your infinite power and genuine abundance. Take a moment and imagine how it feels like. Your ability to be grounded and to maintain your sense of utter peace is right here, right now.

Focus your attention on where you are in this current moment of your physical body, your emotional self, and your spiritual energy. Breathe in with awareness to allow for forgiveness. Breathe out radiating positive energy to the universe. As you are inhaling, feel the gratitude entering your body and showering you with its intensity. While exhaling, feel your ego slipping away. Let go of that ego. Bring awareness to the base of your spine, where your root chakra resides. Inhale deeply into your lower belly and tightly squeeze the area right below your navel. Exhale and feel the energy rising from your root chakra to your crown chakra. This will awaken your seven energy centers and let the energy flow through them.

Your body and your mind are both awake and they are ready to receive what the universe holds for them. Your spiritual calling has been met with absolute success. Even if you were hesitant at first, you begin to realize that you can connect with the universe on a

87

deeper level. You are surrounded by the omnipresent energy that governs everything. It is in your hand to take the next step towards spiritual growth. After visualizing your guide, you can call upon them whenever you wish to explore the universe. A whole new world has unveiled before your eyes and you are ready to take on the challenge of discovering this spectacular gift.

Resume your breathing. With this process, you establish a deeper connection to your soul that brings you to the fulfillment of your deepest desires. It attracts you to your higher purpose, by bringing you to your ultimate sanctuary. It leads you to a place where you feel 100% safe and secure, a place within you where you feel more beautiful than anywhere else in the entire universe. Through this meditation, you can open up to spirituality and learn how to be receptive to the magnificent things that have been destined for you. Take a last deep inhale and as you exhale open your eyes gently.

GUIDED MEDITATION TO OVERCOME FEAR

If you are finding it hard to ease your mind and let go of the fear you are experiencing, then you can turn to this guided meditation. Through this session, you will be able to let go of the anxiety and shift your mindset to withstand the pressure you deal with in your life. By the end of this meditation, you will definitely feel lighter and more hopeful, less stressed, and more focused on the positive aspects of your life.

Sit comfortably and close your eyes. Take some deep breaths, breathing in through your nose and out through your mouth. Focus on your breathing and feel your body calming down slowly. I know you have been experiencing certain negative feelings that have been holding you back. I want you to notice those feelings. There may be some tightening in your chest or a quickening of your heart rates. As you continue through this session, you will feel your heart rates settle and a wonderful sense of inner calm slowly embracing you.

SPIRITUAL GROWTH FOR WOMEN

Repeat the following positive affirmations and feel the powerful weight of each of these affirmations as you repeat them:

"As I breathe in and out, I am aware of my breath. I am aware of my heartbeat. I am aware of my body. As I breathe in and out, I am aware of the anxiety within me. I am aware of my fears. I am aware of any tightness in my chest and any quickening in my heart rates. As I breathe in and out, I acknowledge my negative thoughts and I am well aware of them. Now I calm my negative thoughts. Now I release my negative thoughts. As I breathe in and out, I calm my anxiety. I calm my fears and I relax my mind. I relax my body and I slow down my thoughts. As I breathe in and out, I release my fears. I become free of my anxiety. I become free of suffering. I let go."

You should now feel a wonderful sense of calmness in your body and mind. You are now liberated and free. Invite your mind and your body to drift in a calm state. Notice how relaxed you have become. Within your relaxed awareness, slowly scan your entire body. Allow your awareness to move over each part of your body and observe those parts that were tensed and tightened before. Are they still tight and tensed? You can now rest assured that your body is safe and supported. Allow yourself to go deeper into relaxation.

Acknowledge the fact that your experience can have a powerful effect of being able to soften and release that which you are holding on to. You have the ability to come home to yourself any time you need, by simply connecting with your breath and the sensations within your physical body with love and kindness have the power to relax your nervous system. Find comfort in your entire body now. Your nervous system is shifting and so are you. You have created change and you are now in a very calm state of relaxation. Stay with the experience of your sensations in this tranquility. You can always return to that state of grounded calmness and slow your mind down because it has always been a part of you.

You can stay in this joyful state for as long as you like. It is a safe place for you. You are familiar with this place and therefore it triggers no stress or other negative emotions. When you are ready to

89

ANGELA GRACE

come back, begin to broaden your awareness outwards. Sense the air around you as it makes subtle contact with any exposed part of your body. Open your eyes gently and slightly move your fingers and toes. Take a few deep breaths as you are regaining consciousness of your surroundings and let go of any remaining tension. With every breath, exhale even the tiniest fraction of anxiety and stress from within your body.

Observe your body and see how you feel. Are you still tense, anxious, or tightened? Are you still driven by your fears? As you practice this meditation, you will notice that your fears become milder and less intimidating. You are no longer overwhelmed by those fears. Your stress and anxiety have diminished. Go through the meditation as often as you feel like it, so as to loosen up and become more conscious of absolute serenity all around you. It will help you conquer your fears and eventually overcome them while maintaining a healthy mindset.

11

THE 30-MINUTE DAILY EMPOWERMENT RITUAL FOR SPIRITUAL GROWTH

It is of paramount importance to establish a healthy daily routine that enables you to be proactive in your life, rather than reactive. You should make sure that you have everything you need, in order to wake up energized and filled with gratitude, ready to take on the challenges of the day and thrive. If you are determined to reach those spiritual heights and become a beacon of light and energy, you must prepare yourself for a ritual you can adhere to every single day. Don't just hit the "snooze" button and then wake up scrolling through your phone, looking at other people's social media accounts. This gets you nowhere close to where you want to be.

Instead, be proactive and organize your day exactly as you want. Take time to wake up in the morning and do not rush into anything. If you are an early bird, this is going to be easy. Even if you are not, however, you can still modify your routine and commit to waking up just a little earlier than you used to. Over time, you are going to love this habit. Typically, everything is quieter in the morning and time seems to get by slowly. This offers you the opportunity to do the things you would love to do within the day, but somehow you

ANGELA GRACE

cannot find the time to devote to yourself. Well, from now on you will make time to treat yourself that way and wake up blissfully.

One crucial thing for you to take care of is your bedroom. This is your sanctuary and you must feel safe within it. Keep it clean and decluttered. Nothing hinders your spiritual growth like energy blocks within your personal space. Therefore, you must be thorough when cleaning your room and tidying up. Be sure to get rid of anything that does not spark joy within your life. Sometimes we pile on things that we never use, simply because we neglect to throw them away or we feel sort of attached to them for no reason. Do not pay attention to the materialistic world that much. They are just items. They serve their purpose and we should be grateful for that. However, once they have served their purpose, you should throw them away or better yet donate them to charity.

As soon as you wake up in the morning, I suggest that you open the curtains or the blinds and let that sunshine in. Even if it is not a sunny day, you will still get that boost of light bathing your room. This will have an immediate impact on your mood and it will help you wake up more naturally. Of course, you should also open the windows and let the fresh air in. Any stagnant energy will be gone and new crisp air will flow through your room. What a lovely way of waking up! Now, it is important to maintain your personal space clean and tidy. This is why you need to make your bed right away. There are two reasons for that. First of all, when you make the bed you do not get tempted to crawl back inside. Second, you tidy up and at the same time, you complete your first task within the day so early in the morning.

Dedicate the time to your personal hygiene, washing your face with crisp water that wakes you up and keeps you grounded. You can also shower, depending on your daily routine. After that, you can go and make yourself a nice cup of herbal tea or coffee. Take the time to enjoy your breakfast, just being present in the moment. In a society that has been running wild, even the slightest time to ourselves might be deemed as an unnecessary luxury. Yet, it is a

SPIRITUAL GROWTH FOR WOMEN

much-needed escape from reality. This is a magnificent opportunity to regain balance between your body, your mind, and your spirit. Prepare a healthy breakfast and enjoy.

Below you can see the 30-minute spiritual growth daily ritual secret formula I have created for you. In this ritual, you will find an easy-to-do, simple yet effective way to supercharge your day and promote spiritual growth. Implement these positive notes in your everyday life and you will feel amazing every single morning, be it sunshine or rain. By following such a ritual, you will ease yourself into a state of spiritual awareness and welcome all those wonderful things that you are about to receive. Good morning, everyone!

THE 30-MINUTE SPIRITUAL GROWTH DAILY RITUAL SECRET FORMULA

As stated above, it is essential that you wake up early in the morning. I know that we do not all have the same program. Some work night shifts and some have to work overtime. There are women breastfeeding or taking care of a large family. Regardless of your status, though, you really need to appreciate those moments of absolute peace and quiet in the world. So schedule your alarm clock for 30 minutes prior to your usual morning routine and set out on a unique and joyful experience.

Open the windows and the curtains, make your bed and wash your face, as discussed earlier. Go to the kitchen and get yourself a tall glass of water. This will keep you hydrated and allow you to feel grounded, totally connected to the world. Return to your room and focus on your breathing. Sit down comfortably with your legs crossed and your palms on your lap facing upwards. Take deep breaths, inhaling through the nose and exhaling through the mouth. In this way, you welcome the fresh air in your lungs and you fill your body with new, fresh energy. This first step of your ritual should take about 5 minutes.

Stretch for a few moments to ease your body into the busy day

ANGELA GRACE

ahead. Feel those muscles loosen, become relaxed, and awakened. You can bend your neck on either side of your body, get your arms over your head and then stand up. Bring your hands straight up on top of your head and then gently bring them down along with your torso until you touch your toes with your fingertips. Through stretching, you become aware of your body and you prepare yourself for any activity that might follow. Approximately 3 to 5 minutes of stretching are enough on a daily basis.

The next step is for you to practice gratitude. Give thanks for all the blessings that you have already received in your life. Be grateful for your achievements, for the people around you, and for your ability to wake up in the morning and face another day. You can write in a journal or you can use positive affirmations to express your gratitude. Everyone is grateful for different things in life, but you are free to use any of the following affirmations in your morning ritual:

- I am grateful for the love and acceptance I receive daily.
- I am empowered by the loving people around me.
- I am loveable, I give and receive love unconditionally.
- My friends and family support me in everything I choose to do.
- I love the world, I am part of the world and I am in perfect harmony with the world.
- I am a part of the universe and I am fully aligned to the cosmic balance.
- I feel gratitude for being healthy and happy in my life.
- I receive all my blessings with gratitude and grace.
- I am grateful for being given another chance to live my life.
- I am thankful for being alive and enjoying the wonders of the cosmos.
- Thank you for the blessings this new day is about to give me.

SPIRITUAL GROWTH FOR WOMEN

- I am grateful for the loving, healthy body that I have.
- The universe drives me every day and guides me to my spiritual growth and I am grateful for this.
- My day begins and ends with gratitude.
- My life is filled with happiness and abundance.
- I am free of fear and filled with gratitude.
- Today I attract a deeper love and appreciation for myself.
- I am enough, I am worthy and I am abundantly blessed.
- I am grateful for life and for all the beauty in it.
- I live every day to my fullest potential and I am grateful for that.

Repeat those affirmations out loud and notice how they make you feel. Your vibration will be elevated as you are taking in the concepts of these wonderful sentences and what they represent in your life. You want to be empowered and open up yourself for the spiritual growth you have anticipated all this time. Through these affirmations, you become more receiving of the gifts you are about to be given by the higher power and this is amazing. This step should also take you 5 minutes.

Following your gratitude list, you should indulge in an EFT tapping session to cleanse your aura and raise your vibration. As a result, you will become aware of your spirituality and you will feel deeply connected with the universe. You will release any stagnant energy that has been blocking your growth and you will feel unstoppable. What you need to do is start tapping the various meridian points within your body and repeating positive affirmations that allow you to raise your vibration and reach those elevated spiritual heights. Begin with your palm and move all the way up to the crown of your head. Then move downwards and tap your third eye chakra, which is located right between your eyebrows. Tap also your cheekbones, the area right beside your cartilage and your upper lip, your chin and your throat. Then tap your neckline and the middle of your chest, finishing your round of tapping with the area below your

ANGELA GRACE

armpits. As soon as you complete one round, go ahead and repeat twice more.

What you are saying during your EFT tapping is equally important to your tapping sequence. So you should repeat the following: "*I choose to love and accept myself. I love and accept myself unconditionally. I choose to raise my vibration and I choose to really love and honor myself. I choose to be buzzing with energy. It is my choice to raise my vibration and feel that shot of energy flow through my body. I choose to deeply and completely love and accept myself. More than that, I choose to love and accept everybody else around me. This will help me raise my vibration even more. I am raising my vibration and I am already buzzing with energy. I have so many things to do today and I am finding the energy to do them really well. I will do them as effectively as possible, as efficiently as possible. I am getting things done and I choose to feel really good in the process. I am clearing whatever might bring me down. I am clearing my fears and negative thoughts and I am releasing them from my system. Everything is energy and I am completely filled with energy. I am raising my vibration, feeling this energy in every single fiber of my being. I know that I can do great things. I am giving myself the freedom to do great things and just feel wonderful throughout the day. I deserve that.*"

Take a deep breath and feel that energy shift within your body. You are oozing with energy and it feels like you are indestructible right now. Over time, you will experience the optimal benefits of EFT tapping in your life. That raise of vibration will follow you throughout the day, enabling you to conquer your goals and attract all those magnificent things in your life. You don't have an infinite supply of days and therefore you should celebrate each and every opportunity you are given to show the world what you are truly made of. This step will take you about 10 minutes to complete.

Finally, take a moment and plan your day, thinking of what you are going to achieve. Set your mind on your daily goals and make everyday matter. Visualize those goals as part of your daily routine. Picture in the slightest detail what you are going to do next, what

SPIRITUAL GROWTH FOR WOMEN

you are planning to accomplish, and how you are going to do that. Be specific and experience this visualization as if you are already there. You have already achieved those goals and you are feeling the joy and satisfaction of having conquered yet another fort. How wonderful it feels to get what you want and see as those dreams of yours are brought to life. This final step should take about 5 minutes, bringing you to a total of thirty minutes.

Boil some water and make yourself a nice warm cup of tea or coffee. Sit there in silence, sipping on that liquid bliss and just being present. Prepare an avocado toast, a green smoothie, yogurt with fruit and granola, whatever your heart desires for getting enough energy for the day. Remember that this ritual is your way to start the day on your own terms. It is the only time when you can relax and enjoy precious moments with yourself, structuring the rest of the day beforehand and planning it out exactly the way you want it to unfold. By doing so, you take control over your life and you prepare yourself for what is about to happen. Having completed this ritual, you will definitely feel fuller and more accomplished. You will also feel pumped with energy and ready to go get them!

Nighttime Ritual

After a full day of hard work, endless tasks that require your attention, and urgent matters that just won't go away unless you tackle them, it is time to relax. This is your time to let go of the tension that has accumulated throughout the day and feels good about yourself and your accomplishments. I would advise you to abstain from your TV, laptop, or any other blue light electronic device. In this way, you will have the chance to avoid messing with your circadian rhythms. This will help you get a great night's sleep, which is absolutely necessary for you to remain healthy, happy, and balanced in your life. Rest is of paramount importance and therefore you should never underestimate the power and dynamics of high-quality sleep.

Take a soothing shower and let the water wash away any nega-

ANGELA GRACE

tive energy. You can use essential oils that stimulate your senses in the shower, lifting your spirit through marvelous aromas that fill the room with bliss. After you are done, go ahead with the rest of your beauty routine and self-care. Put on your night cream, hydrate your skin and take care of your body. Next, you may want to get yourself a warm cup of herbal tea or chamomile. This will allow you to relax even further, loosening your muscles and calming your mind. Take your time and prepare this tea for you just like a ritual, as an act of kindness to yourself.

When you come to the bedroom, you can listen to some soft music that promotes relaxation and even aids in your sleep. There are many different options for you to choose from, including deep sleep music, stress relief, meditation music, or even white noises. Have your pick and let it play in the background. Light some scented candles to create a more relaxing atmosphere. You can use any scents you like, such as lavender, cinnamon, sandalwood, or vanilla. Of course, you can also burn incense with splendid aromas that help you relax and let go of the tension. Whatever you do, make sure that your bedroom is an inspiring place where great energy flows effortlessly. This is your sanctuary and you deserve to relax deeply.

This is the best time of the day for you to engage in journaling. Write down everything that comes to mind. You can go through the events of the day and point out the highlights. There might be things you are proud of, such as volunteering in an environmental project or helping a person in need. Don't be afraid to brag about your achievements. If you have behaved in a way that you approve and if you have succeeded in something, then you need to acknowledge it and be grateful. If you want, you can make a list of three things that made you proud today. It doesn't have to be anything fancy or complicated. Your list could be something similar to the following:

SPIRITUAL GROWTH FOR WOMEN

- I am proud of talking kindly to the person in front of me at the bank.
- I am proud of keeping my calm under pressure at the office today.
- I am proud of managing to eat healthily and mindfully, avoiding junk food and soda.

This is a brief reminder of how awesome you are. Obviously, there will be days when your accomplishments are significantly bigger and they will deserve an even deeper acknowledgment. However, every day you should celebrate your victories. No matter how small or trivial they might seem to you, they are always victories and you should be proud of them. Instead of shying away from recognition, you need to accept that you are worthy of praise.

Along with writing down what good you have done, you can also refer to any type of behavior you would rather change. For instance, you can write down that you didn't speak out when your boss asked you your honest opinion about a product, even though you wanted to express your concerns. Do that in a non-judgmental manner that leads to a healthy look at your life. As a result, you can promote a change in your behavioral patterns based on this recollection of your past behavior.

Whenever you are feeling down, you can always turn to your journal and read through all the magnificent things you have accomplished in your life so far. For those who are feeling more creative, you can also draw sketches and create lovely handcrafted items to include within this journal. Pick a notebook that you are fond of, so that you can always spark with joy when you open it. Keep it by your bedside table, in order to have access to it whenever you want to. Get a lovely pen or pencil and you are ready to start writing the book of your life.

Besides journaling, your nighttime ritual should also include some mindful meditation. This is a beautiful way to delve into your spiritual self and wander off before you drift away in your dreams.

ANGELA GRACE

Get comfortable in a restful position and relax. Take a nice, slow, deep breath in and fill your lungs with fresh air. As you exhale, feel the air leave your body completely. Repeat those deep breaths that enable you to become aware of your stillness. Let that breathing ground you to the present moment. You are present at this very moment. let go of everything else you were consumed with throughout the day. there is nowhere else you need to be. There is nothing else you should be doing right now. Give your mind permission right now to wind down and fully rest.

Continue to take slow deep breaths. As you do, feel the entire journey of the breath through your body, breathing in and out of every single muscle and every single cell, from head to toe. Become aware of any parts within your body where you are holding on to tension, anxiety, and stress. Notice any parts within your body that may be sore or tight. Begin breathing into them, so as to dissolve any negative feeling. Unclench your jaw, open your palms, stretch your body to release the tension, and breathe deeply. Give that tension permission to leave your body and fade away.

Now return to your normal breathing pattern, but allow it to become your anchor as you are falling asleep. Even though we often lie down worried that we do not get enough sleep, this is exactly what we shouldn't be doing. The more we focus on something, the more we are likely to experience it. So avoid concentrating on those negative feelings and thoughts. Instead, draw your attention to a positive intention for tonight's sleep. This positive intention is related to the type of sleep you wish to enjoy. Think of a peaceful, restful sleep that is deep and relaxing. Allow this intention to settle in now and ask those feelings of peace, tranquility, restfulness to emerge and embrace you completely.

This guided meditation will help you fall into a deep sleep that refreshes you fully and enables you to relax and rest without anything interrupting this blissful sleep. If you are having trouble sleeping, then you need to follow a nighttime ritual that relieves you of all the tension and anxiety. This ritual will also eliminate any distractions and ease you into a calming state before sleep. Once you have completed your meditation, take some deep breaths and tuck yourself in bed. You can read a little or listen to an ebook or a motivational speech. I am sure that you are going to love this nighttime ritual, as much as the precious sleep you get to enjoy!

AFTERWORD

You have made it to the end of this book and I could not be prouder of you for your perseverance and devotion! I hope that you have found the answers that you have anticipated to get, along with some others that have not yet crossed your mind on the topic. Spiritual growth is a challenging subject and it requires a lot of your energy, time, and dedication. You cannot expect to get the desirable results from one moment to the next. However, the fact that you have bought this book and finished it so eagerly shows me that you are on the right track for greatness.

I have created a book that helps you discover all the different aspects that are relevant to spiritual growth and self-awareness. In these chapters, I have tried to fit as much information as possible about how to shift your mindset and welcome all these wonderful things that are waiting for you in the future. Life is filled with precious treasures and you are welcome to explore them while taking care of yourself and finding out how to heal, soothe the mind, and progress. It is a magnificent journey that you have embarked on and I wish you all the best. I am sure you are going to nail every single day of your life.

I know it can be hard to overcome the boundaries that have

AFTERWORD

been distracting you all this time, preventing you from reaching your higher self. There are negative people surrounding each and every single one of us and it can be difficult to let go of these energy vampires, these narcissists, these people who have learned that it is alright to feed on other people's energy. Such people might be closer than you think. They can be your parents or siblings, your lovers or BFFs, your colleagues or your bosses, they can even be people you have just met at the grocery store or at a nightclub. It is your duty to identify them and get rid of them as soon as possible. Cut the cord until they rot you from the inside with their toxicity.

Holding on to grudges and seeking revenge is perhaps the worst thing you can do in your life. I am aware of the hostility and cruelty harboring in the heart of certain people. It is inexplicable to some, but it is true that goodness and cruelty are not that far apart. To be honest, when a person behaves badly to me, I almost feel pity for them. They don't know any better. This is how they have been raised to act and feel. However, you should not behave in the same way. By being revengeful, what you do essentially is prevent you from reaching your higher self. You are consumed in negative emotions that get to poison you from within, offering nothing in return.

What you need to do instead is forgive. Although your first reaction to this is definitely going to be negative, I cannot stress enough just how vital forgiveness is to your physical and mental health. It frees you from the burden of having to hold on to something so negative that you cannot even breathe. Unless you resolve the conflict and get closure, you can never be expected to find peace. Even if you have no control over the things that other people do to you, it is true that you have control over how you react to those things. It is entirely up to you if you continue to be the victim or not. Forgive even if you do not forget. In this way, you will see that the power that trigger had on you will slowly vanish into thin air.

Life can be hard on so many different levels. It is not all roses and flowers and it is definitely not like a walk in the park. Still, you

AFTERWORD

need to persevere. You should never give up. Every day you wake up and you are healthy, you are given an invaluable gift. You are given the opportunity to seize that day and take full advantage of its potential. Why would you ever throw this gift away? We have been given a specific supply of new days in our lives. No matter how persistent we are, there is no refill. Therefore, you must be mindful as to how you wish to spend these days. You must think carefully about what you want to make of them and how you want others to remember you.

You have the power to change your life and you need to believe in this. There is no room for doubting yourself and always putting other people's lives first. You are a unique human being with infinite power, radiant energy, and the possibility to achieve greatness in your life. Why would you self-sabotage and hinder your progress simply because you have been taught to sacrifice for others? This is not an act of kindness, rather than an act of cruelty to yourself and the community. As soon as you realize that your life is just as important as the rest within your family and loved ones, you can grow spiritually and accomplish everything you have wanted in life. As soon as you have taken care of yourself, you will be strong enough to help others and contribute to the world.

In this book, I have also wanted to address a huge issue that can make a person's life unbearable. Depression is one of the worst feelings and it can take over your life without even noticing. There will be signs, but it is hard for you to catch on to these red flags and act accordingly. Hopefully, you will find a way to crush depression and regain your mental power and I will be overwhelmed if I can help even a little in this battle of yours with the beast!

Ultimately, I want to thank you for taking the time and reading my book. It is an absolute honor. I am positive that you are going to love those guided meditations, morning and nighttime rituals, as well as other practical information that helps you supercharge your self-growth. Enjoy and take care, stay blessed and be as beautiful as you are radiant!

REFERENCES

Ackerman, C. E. (2018, May). *Self-Fulfilling Prophecy in Psychology: 10 Examples and Definition (+PDF)*. PositivePsychology.com. https://positivepsychology.com/self-fulfilling-prophecy/

"Aura Photography - How to Read Aura Photos." *Goop*, 19 Mar. 2015, goop.com/wellness/spirituality/radiant-human-aura-photography/.

Berzins, Zigmar. "Women Jetty Lake," *Pixabay*, 2 Nov. 2016, pixabay.com/photos/women-jetty-lake-pier-fashion-1784755/.

David, Jackson. "Freedom Girl Travel," *Pixabay*, 22 Jan. 2020, pixabay.com/photos/freedom-girl-travel-adventure-4782870/.

Dotigabrielf. "Portrait Women Vintage," *Pixabay*, 11 Apr. 2017, pixabay.com/photos/portrait-women-vintage-photography-2218882/.

Fields, L. (2003, February 7). *What is OCD?* WebMD; WebMD. https://www.webmd.com/mental-health/obsessive-compulsive-disorder#1

Forotech. "Sky Freedom Happiness," *Pixabay*, 2017, pixabay.com/photos/sky-freedom-happiness-relieved-2667455/.

Giordano, Nicola. "Woman Riding Horse," *Pixabay*, 26 May 2018, pixabay.com/photos/woman-riding-horse-animals-mare-3432069/.

REFERENCES

Graphix, Shift. "Sadness Depressed Woman," *Pixabay*, 28 May 2018, pixabay.com/photos/sadness-depressed-woman-girl-alone-3434515/.

Hassan, Mohamed. "Meditating Sunset Meditation," *Pixabay*, 17 June 2018, pixabay.com/photos/meditating-sunset-meditation-yoga-3478898/.

J, Ana. "Girl Sea Beach," *Pixabay*, 28 Aug. 2014, pixabay.com/photos/girl-sea-beach-young-summer-429380/.

Jeffrey, Scott. "A Closer Look at Carl Jung's Individuation Process: A Map for Psychic Wholeness." *Scott Jeffrey*, 11 Jan. 2019, scottjeffrey.com/individuation-process/.

K, Larisa. "Tree Flowers Meadow," *Pixabay*, 27 Feb. 2014, pixabay.com/photos/tree-flowers-meadow-tree-trunk-276014/.

Luenen, Michael. "Freedom Live Love," *Pixabay*, 3 Jan. 2020, pixabay.com/photos/freedom-live-love-nature-cliffs-4737919/.

Mayo Clinic Staff. (2018, July 6). *Post-traumatic stress disorder (PTSD) - Symptoms and causes.* Mayo Clinic; Mayo Clinic. https://www.mayoclinic.org/diseases-conditions/post-traumatic-stress-disorder/symptoms-causes/syc-20355967

Pexels. "Countryside Crop," *Pixabay*, 21 Nov. 2016, pixabay.com/photos/countryside-crop-cropland-farm-1845693/.

Photos, Free. "Girl Brave Bravery," *Pixabay*, 15 July 2015, pixabay.com/photos/girl-brave-bravery-independence-843076/.

Photos, Free. "Woman Profile Face," *Pixabay*, 27 Mar. 2015, pixabay.com/photos/woman-profile-face-portrait-young-690118/.

Schicker, A. (2013, February 5). *What Is PROCRASTINATION and How Can You Overcome It?* Procrastination.com; Procrastination.com. https://procrastination.com/what-is-procrastination

Sergo. "Wild Flowers Tea," *Pixabay*, 16 June 2020, pixabay.com/photos/wild-flowers-tea-in-the-field-5303044/.

Silviarita. "Young Woman Girl," *Pixabay*, 31 Aug. 2017, pixabay.com/photos/young-woman-girl-sporty-nature-2699780/.

Snap, Stock. "People Woman Happy," *Pixabay*, 3 Aug. 2017, pixabay.com/photos/people-woman-happy-enjoy-smile-2575901/.

REFERENCES

Tentis, Dana. "Woman Beautiful Girl," *Pixabay*, 23 Jan. 2017, pixabay.com/photos/woman-beautiful-girl-lying-leaves-2003647/.

Voicu, Adina. "Girl Flowers Model," *Pixabay*, 12 Apr. 2016, pixabay.com/photos/girl-flowers-model-lying-down-1319114/.

Wellington, Jill. "Sunflowers Field Woman," *Pixabay*, 30 Aug. 2018, pixabay.com/photos/sunflowers-field-woman-yellow-3640938/.

Zborilova, Sofie. "Girl Woman Portrait," *Pixabay*, 15 June 2018, pixabay.com/photos/girl-woman-portrait-smile-blonde-3475673/.

YOUR FEEDBACK IS VALUED

We would like to be so bold as to ask for an act of kindness from you. If you read and enjoyed our book/s, would you please consider leaving an honest review on Amazon or audible? As an independent publishing group, your feedback means the absolute world to us. We read every single review we receive and would love to hear your thoughts, as each piece of feedback helps us serve you better. Your feedback may also impact others across the globe, helping them discover powerful knowledge they can implement in their lives to give them hope and self-empowerment. Wishing you empowerment, courage, and wisdom on your journey.

If you have read or listened to any of our books and would be so kind as to review them, you can do so by clicking the 'learn more' tab under the book's picture on our website:

https://ascendingvibrations.net/books

YOUR FEEDBACK IS VALUED

Why not join our Facebook community and discuss your spiritual path with like-minded seekers?

We would love to hear from you!

Go here to join the 'Ascending Vibrations' community:
bit.ly/ascendingvibrations

YOUR BONUS AUDIOBOOK IS READY

Download the 6+ Hour Audiobook *'Divine Feminine Energy (Manifesting for Women & Feminine Energy Awakening - 2 in 1 Collection)'* Instantly for **FREE!**

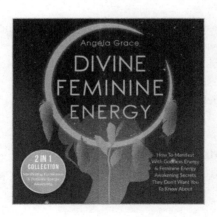

If you love listening to audio books on-the-go, I have great news for you. You can download the audio book version of *'Divine Feminine Energy'* for **FREE** just by signing up for a **FREE** 30-day audible trial! See below for more details!

YOUR BONUS AUDIOBOOK IS READY

Audible trial benefits

As an audible customer, you'll receive the below benefits with your 30-day free trial:

- Free audible copy of this book
- After the trial, you will get 1 credit each month to use on any audiobook
- Your credits automatically roll over to the next month if you don't use them
- Choose from over 400,000 titles
- Listen anywhere with the audible app across multiple devices
- Make easy, no hassle exchanges of any audiobook you don't love
- Keep your audiobooks forever, even if you cancel your membership
- And much more

Go to the links below to get started:
Go here for AUDIBLE US: bit.ly/divinefeminineenergy
Go here for AUDIBLE UK: bit.ly/divinefeminineenergyuk

Made in the USA
Las Vegas, NV
12 March 2024

87082218R00080